KU-468-986

PAUL SPICKER

WHAT'S WRONG WITH SOCIAL SECURITY BENEFITS?

POLICY PRESS SHORTS INSIGHTS

First published in Great Britain in 2017 by

Policy Press
University of Bristol
1-9 Old Park Hill
Bristol
BS2 8BB
UK
t: +44 (0)117 954 5940
pp-info@bristol.ac.uk
www.policypress.co.uk

North America office:
Policy Press
c/o The University of Chicago Press
1427 East 60th Street
Chicago, IL 60637, USA
t: +1 773 702 7700
f: +1 773 702 9756
sales@press.uchicago.edu
www.press.uchicago.edu

© Paul Spicker 2017

British Library Cataloguing in Publication Data
A catalogue record for this book is available from the British Library.

Library of Congress Cataloging-in-Publication Data
A catalog record for this book has been requested.

ISBN 978-1-4473-3732-4 (paperback)
ISBN 978-1-4473-3734-8 (ePub)
ISBN 978-1-4473-3735-5 (Mobi)
ISBN 978-1-4473-3733-1 (ePDF)

The right of Paul Spicker to be identified as author of this work has been asserted by him in accordance with the Copyright, Designs and Patents Act 1988.

All rights reserved: no part of this publication may be reproduced, stored in a retrieval system, or transmitted in any form or by any means, electronic, mechanical, photocopying, recording, or otherwise without the prior permission of Policy Press.

The statements and opinions contained within this publication are solely those of the authors and not of the University of Bristol or Policy Press. The University of Bristol and Policy Press disclaim responsibility for any injury to persons or property resulting from any material published in this publication.

Policy Press works to counter discrimination on grounds of gender, race, disability, age and sexuality.

Cover design by Policy Press
Front cover: image kindly supplied by Getty
Printed and bound in Great Britain by CMP, Poole
Policy Press uses environmentally responsible print partners

Contents

List of tables and figures

About the author

Paul Spicker is Emeritus Professor of Public Policy at the Robert Gordon University, Aberdeen, and a Fellow of the International Social Science Council's Comparative Research Group on Poverty (CROP). His research includes studies of poverty, need, disadvantage and service delivery; he has worked as a consultant for a range of agencies in social welfare. His books include:

- *Stigma and social welfare* (Croom Helm, 1984)
- *Principles of social welfare* (Routledge, 1988)
- *Social housing and the social services* (Longmans, 1989)
- *Poverty and social security: Concepts and principles* (Routledge, 1993)
- *Planning for the needs of people with dementia* (with D.S. Gordon) (Avebury, 1997)
- *Social protection: A bilingual glossary* (co-editor with J.-P. Révauger) (Mission-Recherche, 1998)
- *Social policy in a changing society* (with Maurice Mullard) (Routledge, 1998)
- *Policy analysis for practice* (The Policy Press, 2006)
- *Poverty: An international glossary* (co-editor with Sonia Alvarez Leguizamon and David Gordon) (Zed, 2007)
- *The welfare state: A general theory* (Sage, 2000)
- *Liberty, equality and fraternity* (The Policy Press, 2006)
- *The idea of poverty* (The Policy Press, 2007)
- *The origins of modern welfare* (Peter Lang, 2010)
- *How social security works* (The Policy Press, 2011)
- *Reclaiming individualism* (The Policy Press, 2013)
- *Social policy: Theory and practice* (The Policy Press, 2014)
- *Arguments for welfare* (Rowman and Littlefield, 2017)

A range of his published work is available on open access at:
http://spicker.uk

ONE

Understanding social security

This book is about benefits in Britain. Its purpose is to suggest some small improvements that might be made in the operation of the benefits system. To do that, it needs to explain a little about how benefits work, where the system seems to be going wrong and what might be done about it.[1]

The system of cash benefits is usually referred to as 'social security', but there is a lot of confusion about the term. Benefits work by paying money to people so that they can go out and buy things. Typical examples are pensions, unemployment benefits, disability benefits and payments to families for children. 'Social security' is the name for the whole system of benefits. That is not the only way the term is used, however. In the US, 'social security' refers only to the public system of social insurance benefits, mainly for older people and some people with disabilities. In France, '*la sécurité sociale*' includes provision for health care. A range of other terms are used for benefits in other places: 'social protection', 'income maintenance', 'welfare'.

Some cash payments do not get counted as social security. Single Farm Payment, paid to UK farmers, is treated as something completely

[1] Thanks for comments are due to Gareth Morgan and to Malcolm Torry, who commented on the section on universal basic income. The views expressed are my own and the mistakes, of course, are mine.

different. Civil service pensions are treated as a private occupational scheme, not a benefit payment. Legal aid, paid to lawyers, is thought of quite differently from Housing Benefit, often paid to landlords. Some occasional payments of cash to social work clients tend not to be seen as part of the social security system.

On the other hand, there are benefits that do count as social security but are not given in cash. Council Tax Reduction is paid by reducing the bill for council tax that someone would have to pay otherwise. Free milk and vitamins, given to expectant mothers, are usually treated as part of the benefits system, though they could just as easily have been classified as health care. Some benefit systems use vouchers or pass cards; some local authorities have been using supermarket cards so that people cannot take the money and use it how they please.

This may all look a bit of a muddle, and indeed it is. The benefits system is complicated. It deals with a huge range of different circumstances and contingencies. There are lots of benefits. The complexity can be seen in the range of conditions that they are responding to, the often puzzling criteria for eligibility, the convoluted rules and the interactions between benefits.

Why pay benefits?

One of the reasons why benefits are so complex is that they are not generally there to do just one thing – such as helping people who are poor, or redistributing income. Countries which have started out with that kind of simple-minded approach have invariably been pushed in different directions, and find themselves having to do far more. The classic example is the Poor Law Amendment Act of 1834. It was intended to make the most restrictive provision possible for the poor, supposedly safeguarding the relative position of independent workers and reducing any incentive to have illegitimate children. It became the basis, over time, for a system of local government, health and housing.

The aims of social security are many. They overlap, and on occasion they pull in different directions. They include:

- *Humanitarianism and charity.* There is hardly a society in the world where rich people do not give to poor people. Some benefit systems have begun with the desire to be charitable – or to organise charity so that it can be done without undesirable side-effects.
- *The relief of poverty.* Some benefits are designed to specifically help poor people. Social assistance is sometimes just about money; sometimes, it is tied in with social work to integrate poor people with the rest of society.
- *Meeting need.* Meeting needs is not just about poverty. There are benefits for people with disabilities that try to meet the extra costs of disability. There are benefits for health and education in order to make sure that people are able to use these services without suffering financial penalties.
- *Insurance.* In many countries, social security did not begin with the state. People buy insurance because it is a way of protecting themselves when bad things happen: for example, they may want to protect their families if they die.
- *Social protection.* Social protection is an extension of the insurance principle. Anyone can be old, sick, disabled or unemployed; benefits systems commonly provide protection against common social contingencies.
- *Income smoothing.* Social security can act to transfer income from one part of a person's life to another – most obviously, from adulthood to old age.
- *Redistribution.* Social security is sometimes seen as a way of taking money from one group of people to move it to another – from workers to pensioners, from people with no children to people who do have children, from richer people to poorer people, and so on.
- *Compensation.* Some schemes, such as Industrial Injury Benefit and War Pension, offer compensation for damage suffered.
- *Social inclusion.* There are social security schemes which try to find a place for people in society, partly through money and partly through education, training and creating opportunities for people to participate in society.

- *Behaviour change.* Social security schemes are used to offer incentives or inducements, to reward people for perceived good things (like marriage) and to punish disapproved ones (like idleness). Some benefits for mothers are intended to promote public health. In many developing countries, Conditional Cash Transfers have been used to promote health care and education.
- *Economic management.* Public spending on social security schemes is an important instrument of economic management. Temporary unemployment assistance improves the efficiency of the labour market by giving people time for job searches. Schemes for disability and retirement help the functioning of the labour market by making it possible for people to withdraw from it.
- *Solidarity.* Social security is often seen as promoting a sense of mutual responsibility, of shared rights and obligations, and of social cohesion.
- *Financing particular activities.* Social security has been used, for example, to put money into the provision of residential care and to support the development of low-cost housing.

This list is not exhaustive. Some of the other things that certain benefits are meant to do are very specific: for example, managing medical certification, promoting rehabilitation or diverting redress away from the courts. A pat formula, such as 'work for those who can and support for those who can't', cannot hope to do justice to the situation. Benefits are more than a safety net; they are about more than need; their roles go far beyond the world of work. Part of what has gone wrong with the programme of welfare reform under Labour and reviews of benefits under the Coalition or the Conservatives has been a failure to understand why these benefits are there.

What circumstances are the benefits paid for?

The next thing to consider is what the benefits are paid for. The main classes of benefit are paid to meet certain common contingencies, so the question 'What is the benefit meant to do?' often gets translated into 'Who should get it?'. The most important categories are:

- Old age (for example, State Pension and Pension Credit). The State Pension is conceived partly as a basic income in old age, partly a return for contribution to society and partly a form of redistribution across the life-cycle.
- Disability (Personal Independence Payment or PIP, Industrial Injury Benefit, War Pensions). Disability benefits may compensate people for disadvantage, contribute towards higher costs of living, make allowance for prolonged spells on low incomes and help pay for care needs. Some benefits are a form of insurance; war pensions offer more generous compensation to reflect the deserving status of the recipients.
- Incapacity for work (Employment and Support Allowance or ESA). This is often confused with disability, but it is markedly different. If people are unable to work, there will be income needs; but beyond that, there needs to be a system to excuse them from working to protect their health, the health of others and the efficiency of the employer. Some incapacity benefits have rehabilitative elements.
- Unemployment (Jobseekers Allowance or JSA). Most periods of unemployment are relatively short and JSA is supposed to provide temporary relief, a degree of income smoothing and support for efficient transfers in the labour market. There is a long-standing distinction between insurance-based social protection benefits and means-tested benefits for low incomes; JSA, which has elements of both, was established when it seemed that the previous insurance-based benefit, Unemployment Benefit, had foundered. However, many recent policy measures have been introduced on the questionable premise that without support, unemployment is likely to be long-term.
- Responsibility for children (Child Benefit, Child Tax Credit). Support for children is partly governed by issues of poverty and child deprivation, but the idea of a 'family wage' has arguably been

more influential, adjusting income from other sources to allow for a basic income for families.

- Paying housing costs while on low incomes (mainly Housing Benefit). Housing Benefit was originally introduced in the 1970s in an attempt to replace subsidies for housing by subsidies for low income. Subsequently, its cost has been driven up by a determination to develop private renting as an alternative to public housing. Support for mortgage costs is limited, and will be changed to a system of loans in 2018, but it is still available in Income Support, JSA, ESA and Pension Credit.

- Caring responsibilities (Carer's Allowance). The language of caring is, at times, conflated with issues of disability, but carers are in a distinct position in their own right – often having low income and interruption in earnings but unable to make themselves available for work.

- People with low earnings. There is a long history of using benefits to top up low earnings – it goes back to the out-relief practised in the 18th-century Poor Law, most famously, in the Speenhamland system – but the idea was given a fillip by Milton Friedman's arguments for a negative income tax,[2] and some benefits were introduced in the 1970s that offered benefits to people in work. The main current examples are Tax Credits, Housing Benefit and Council Tax Reduction.

- Bereavement (Bereavement Payment, Widowed Parent's Allowance). There is an argument for insurance to protect survivors and to meet extra costs following a death, and many people buy this protection separately in the private market. The UK system has interpolated other principles (including, until recently, withdrawal of support for women who remarried and more generous provision for middle-aged widows), which were based on an antiquated understanding of the role of the family breadwinner.

---

[2] M. Friedman (1961) *Capitalism and freedom*, Chicago, IL: University of Chicago Press, ch 12.

- Emergencies and crises (local welfare assistance, the Discretionary Assistance Fund in Wales or the Scottish Welfare Fund). The latest schemes allow for very small grants for the destitute and some special expenses (for example, those related to community care).

Some benefits cut across several categories. Maternity benefits are partly justified in terms of the position of children and partly by the need to excuse expecting mothers from the labour market. ESA covers temporary illness and unemployment for disabled people. Working Tax Credit has elements relating to low income, disability and child-care costs. The categories are largely a matter of convention. There used to be benefits or sections of benefits clearly identified for lone parents, for death, for short-term sickness and for people with chronic disabilities who have been unable to contribute – most of these needs are being met, but they are liable to be hidden somewhere within other benefits. There are no benefits specific to self-employed people, part-time workers, young people or people in residential care – they are all dealt with under different heads – but there could be.

Different types of benefit

There are several quite different types of mechanisms by which benefits are calculated and delivered. At the risk of oversimplifying, it is possible to identify six main categories, none of which is without its problems:

- *National Insurance benefits* were introduced as part of the Beveridge system after the Second World War. The State Pension is an insurance benefit: people pay contributions and their entitlement to benefit depends on the contributions they have made. Elements of JSA and ESA still refer to people's contributions.

  National Insurance was intended to be the basis for the whole benefits system, and for nearly fifty years it certainly was the main category of benefits in Britain. It is still substantially the basis of the State Pension, though contributions could variously have come from employment, self-employment, spouses' contributions (now being phased out), credited contributions for periods of unemployment or home responsibility, and voluntary contributions to fill in gaps. The advantages of National Insurance are that the principle is widely understood and accepted (even if the mechanics are baffling), that it raises money very effectively, and that the delivery of benefits is rather simpler than many others. The main disadvantage of National Insurance is that the coverage is necessarily incomplete. The system has always left gaps because some people were not able to make contributions: school leavers, people with disabilities from an early age and mothers who had not worked were particularly likely not to have the contributions they needed. By the time Unemployment Benefit was abolished in favour of JSA, relatively few unemployed people were entitled. The disadvantages are that the contributions are regressive – they take higher proportions from poor people than they do from richer ones. At the same time, because the contributions have to be low enough for most people to afford, and because the Treasury was never ready to put into the scheme the amounts that would be needed to make the funding work, the benefits are ungenerous.

- *Social assistance* offers basic benefits for people who fall below a minimum level of income. These benefits work by paying the minimum if someone has nothing, or topping them up to the minimum if they have something but not enough. This is the basic rule for JSA, ESA and Pension Credit. (It was the rule of National Assistance, Supplementary Benefit and Income Support, but these have been abolished.)

The safety net that these benefits provide was initially supposed to apply only to limited numbers of people, but as time has gone on, it came to apply to millions – not just unemployed people and those too ill to work, but getting on for two million pensioners (not including another three quarters of a million who probably ought to get the minimum income guarantee but don't). Providing a minimum income is important, but the scheme has many faults. Income is difficult to identify and track, mistakes are rife, and many people do not get the benefits they are entitled to (more on this in due course).

- *Tapered benefits* are also means-tested, but they do not pay a fixed minimum. What they do instead is to adjust to the income that a person has coming in, and they are gradually withdrawn as that income increases. Someone on a low income will get more than someone on a higher income. This is the principle behind Housing Benefit, Council Tax Support, Tax Credits and Universal Credit.

   Tapered benefits have never worked well. They are complicated both in conception and in practice. It is extremely difficult for people to work out whether they are entitled, what they are entitled to or – just as important – when their entitlements stop. There is a 'poverty trap': high marginal rates of deduction lead to people gaining little or no advantage from efforts to improve their income. Take-up of most benefits has been consistently poor, with the apparent exception of Tax Credits – despite them being condemned by the Ombudsman as being fundamentally unsuited to the needs of low-income families.[3]

- *Non-contributory benefits* are paid without a test of means or contributions, but they may have a test of need. Attendance Allowance and Disability Living Allowance (DLA) are selected on the basis of a test of capacity. War Disablement Pension and Industrial Injury Benefit work to similar criteria.

   Several non-contributory benefits were introduced in the 1970s, in the belief that they would avoid the stigma and administrative problems of means-tested benefits for people with disabilities. This was a forlorn hope: the tests are intrusive, people's understanding of the benefits has never been strong and take-up remains poor.

- *Universal benefits* are provided for broad categories of people. Child Benefit is for children (or, properly speaking, for families that are responsible for dependent children), the State Pension for people over the age of 80 is non-contributory and Winter Fuel

---

[3] Parliamentary and Health Service Ombudsman (2007) *Tax credits – getting it wrong?*, HC 1010, p 5.

Payment is added to benefits for a range of people without a test of contribution or need.

Universal services are relatively simple, much easier to administer than selective services and widely accepted – examples are the universal system of education and the health service. Universal benefits are often seen as expensive and badly targeted. Whether either of those charges is true depends on how broadly the eligibility criteria are defined: a universal funeral grant would not be very expensive (funerals are one-off payments for a defined group of people), but a universal working-age income would be.

- *Discretionary benefits* are paid in special circumstances. Examples are local welfare assistance (in England) or the Scottish Welfare Fund, paid by local authorities, or the payments that are made by social workers to help clients in urgent need. Discretionary payments have had a bad press, because they are typically used by (or refused to) people in desperate circumstances. However, every social security system needs to have some provision of this kind; it becomes a matter of concern when people have to rely on help of this sort because their basic benefits are inadequate to manage day to day.

There is an argument for breaking down this list still further, or finding new categories – such as tax reliefs, lump-sum payments by the courts, statutory sick pay or redundancy payments – but these are the main options.

Table 1.1 does not summarise everything in the last two sections, but it helps to show something of the complexity that they imply. Only one of the contingencies – provision for older people – is responded to with every kind of benefit.

Table 1.1: Benefits for people in different circumstances

	Older people	Disability	Incapacity for work	Unemployed	Children	Caring	Low earnings	Bereavement
National Insurance	State Pension		ESA (for six months)	JSA (for six months)	Guardians Allowance			Bereavement payments
Means-tested – minimum income	Pension Credit	ESA	ESA	JSA	Income Support (now mainly legacy in JSA)	Income Support with carers premium		
Means-tested – tapered	Housing Benefit Council Tax Support	Working Tax Credit Housing Benefit Council Tax Support	Housing Benefit Council Tax Support Universal Credit	Housing Benefit Council Tax Support Universal Credit	Child Tax Credit		Tax credits Housing Benefit Universal Credit	
Non-contributory with test of need	Attendance Allowance DLA/PIP Personal care (Scotland)	DLA/PIP War Pension				Carer's Allowance		
Universal	Pensions over 80 Winter Fuel Payment				Child Benefit			
Discretionary	Social care	Community care grants			Fostering and adoption payments Social work payments (Scotland)			Funeral grants

TWO

Misunderstanding social security

Over the course of the last few years, many people in Britain have come to accept a series of myths about social security, increasingly referred to as 'welfare'. It is widely believed that:

- spending on social security is out of control;
- people have become dependent on the welfare state;
- there are massive disincentives to work;
- there are families where no one has worked for generations;
- immigrants come to Britain to take advantage of the benefits system; and
- fraud and abuse are rife.

These are 'myths' in the formal sense of that term: they may not be true, but regardless of that, they are so widely believed that they have changed the way that people think and politicians decide about policy.

Spending

The place to start is with the cost of benefits. Figure 2.1 shows the current pattern of spending.[1] There are three main elements. The biggest element is spending on older people – not just for pensions, but for many other benefits. The second biggest element consists of benefits paid through Her Majesty's Revenue and Customs (HMRC), the tax authority – Child Benefit and the Tax Credit scheme, introduced to support people on low incomes in and out of work. The third element is made up of social security benefits for people of working age, mainly provided by the Department for Work and Pensions (DWP).

Figure 2.1: Public spending on benefits

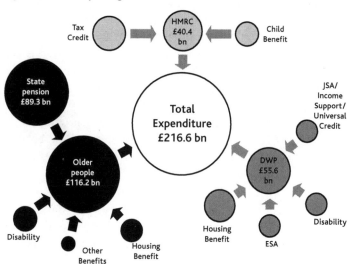

---

[1] Department for Work and Pensions, continuing series, 'Benefit expenditure and caseload tables', available at: https://www.gov.uk/government/collections/benefit-expenditure-tables. Figures are DWP forecasts for 2015-16; they do not tally exactly.

The most obvious thing to say from the figure is that most social security spending is for older people. This is not just down to the State Pension, though that is nearly as big as all the working-age benefits put together; it takes in aspects of several other benefits, including benefits for housing and disability. Looking at the rest, this is not about work. Most of the money is paid to people regardless of whether or not they are in work. Child Benefit, Housing Benefit, Disability Living Allowance (DLA) and Child Tax Credit are paid to people in and out of work. (Housing Benefit and DLA are also paid to older people, which reduces the relative size of the bubbles for 'housing' and 'disability' going to people of working age.) Working Tax Credit is exclusively for people in work; overall, more than 70% of Tax Credits are paid to people in work. There are three main 'out of work' benefits: Employment and Support Allowance (ESA), Jobseekers Allowance (JSA) and Carer's Allowance – Income Support, once the biggest benefit of its type, is being closed down. ESA and its predecessor, Incapacity Benefit, were for people who it was not reasonable to expect to work, and Income Support was for people who were excused from work (lone parents, carers and people with severe disabilities). Only JSA is directly concerned with work; that point might be stretched to include ESA, but even taking those two together, it only makes up a small part of the picture. The overblown emphasis in 'welfare reform' on work and worklessness has surprisingly little to do with what social security is really about.

Is spending out of control? Spending on social security is largely based on entitlements rather than the allocation of a specified budget, and it has never been managed in quite the way that spending on health or education is managed. In health services, the government sets a budget and money is divided between the areas of health, with health-care agencies spending more or less what they have budgeted to spend (often a little more, because the system penalises agencies that cope within their budgets). In social security, the amount paid in pensions and benefits is set year by year, and the actual amount that the government spends will depend on how many people need to claim it – how many old people there are, how many people become sick or disabled, how many become unemployed, and so on. This is largely predictable, but it is not actually 'capped', because there is no mechanism for saying that benefits cannot be paid when the money runs out. (George Osborne, the former Chancellor who introduced the cap, hoped that it might work like this in the future, but the so-called 'welfare cap' has no real force: a government that overspends the cap will have to 'explain', and the explanation is easy – that there are more pensioners, more unemployment or whatever the case may be.)

A better test, then, is whether the cost is increasing. Some bits of the budget have gone up and some have not. There are adjustments to make for inflation, so it makes more sense to look at this as a proportion of the national income. Figure 2.2 shows the pattern of growth of benefits and tax credits from 1979 to the present.

Figure 2.2: Social security spending as a percentage of gross domestic product

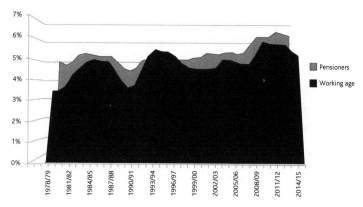

Within those global figures, it is true to say that some benefits have grown disproportionately. The improvement in pensions aside, there are three benefits that have shown a marked increase in the course of the last 15 years or so. One is tax credits, which reflects the spread of low-paid employment; this will be reduced over time with the increases in the minimum wage, and eventually transferred to the Universal Credit scheme. The second is Housing Benefit. This has grown partly because of an increase in private renting, but also because rents in social housing have been deliberately increased to match the private market. A third is DLA, now being replaced by Personal Independence Payment (PIP). The main increase there is down to two factors: the increasing number of claims related to mental illness, and the prolongation of entitlement for older people who can retain the benefit over the maximum age if their claim started early enough. The replacement benefit does nothing to reduce either of those pressures.

Viewing the figures overall, the increase in support for older people, who account for most of the spending, has been steady. There has been an increase in benefits for people of working age, but it has fluctuated and it is not noticeably greater than it was in the mid-1990s. There have been three main periods when more people claimed benefit, and so the benefits cost more: these three periods were (more or less) during 1984–86, 1992–96 and 2008–12. Social security spending goes up during a slump; that is what it was always supposed to do.[2]

The growth of dependency

Most people believe that 'our current welfare system has created a culture of dependency'.[3] The story that has taken hold suggests that the liberal provision of the welfare state has led to people taking advantage: that people choose to live on state handouts. This is from the *Daily Telegraph*:

A system designed as a safety net for the most vulnerable has swelled into an all-consuming client state which stifles aspirations and dignity. The percentage that could be defined as 'dependent' on state provision of some sort or other rose from 46 per cent when Labour took office in 1997 to 52.5 per cent by 2010.

[2] J. Richardson (1960) *Economic and financial aspects of social security*, London: George Allen and Unwin, pp 215–18.

[3] Trades Union Congress (2013) 'Support for benefit cuts dependent on ignorance, TUC-commissioned poll finds', available at: https://www.tuc.org.uk/social-issues/child-poverty/welfare-and-benefits/tax-credits/support-benefit-cuts-dependent

Under the Coalition, it has fallen marginally to 52 per cent. Clearly, these include both cash payments and benefits-in-kind such as access to education and health care. Also, as the population ages, more older people will be drawing the State Pension. Yet, even looking at non-retired households alone, 38 per cent still claim more in benefits than they pay in taxes. Since the Second World War, in other words, a welfare system established to end privation and act as a safety net for those in difficulties has become all-pervasive.[4]

The starting point for this comment is a mistake. The welfare state was not founded as 'a safety net for the most vulnerable'. There had been a system like that for 350 years beforehand. The Poor Law reserved provision to people who were in the most serious need, and it was generally hated. The British welfare state was intended to be its polar opposite. Asa Briggs, in a classic essay, identified three main ways in which the welfare state operated:

> First by guaranteeing individuals and families a minimum income irrespective of the market value of their work, or their property. Second by narrowing the extent of insecurity by enabling individuals and families to meet certain 'social contingencies' (for example sickness, old age and unemployment) which lead otherwise to individual or family crisis, and third, by ensuring that all citizens without distinction of status or class are offered the best standards available in relation to a certain agreed range of social services.[5]

---

[4] *Daily Telegraph* (2015) 'The destructive effect of dependency on the state', 15 February, available at: http://www.telegraph.co.uk/news/politics/conservative/11414430/The-destructive-effect-of-dependency-on-the-state.html

[5] A. Briggs (1961) 'The welfare state in historical perspective', *European Journal of Sociology*, vol 2, pp 221–58.

There is a world of difference between offering 'the best standards available' to all citizens and providing 'a safety net for the vulnerable'.

In that light, the *Telegraph*'s figures can be read in a very different way. A substantial part of the 'dependency' that they are complaining about is concerned with health, education and security in old age. Some of us might think that collective provision for these things is a good idea. When it comes to people of working age, 38% are net beneficiaries, which presumably means that 62% are not. If that means that the top two-thirds are supporting the bottom third, this is not obviously a problem; most of the population will have passed through the bottom third during the previous ten years,[6] and it seems an eminently sensible way to manage the nation's affairs. It is important to challenge the common assumption that the 38% consists of the same people, year after year – that this is the 'dependent' or 'shameless' population, while decent and respectable folk pay for them. For people in the lower half of the earnings distribution, earnings are increasingly precarious, unstable and unpredictable. John Hills reports that in his research, more than a quarter of families had incomes that went up and down erratically, and two-thirds had major changes in income in the course of a year. He comments: 'People's circumstances, even over quite short periods, do not stay static in a way that is easy for them, still less bureaucratic systems, to cope with.'[7]

Table 2.1 shows the length of time that people have continuously spent on benefit.[8] The balance has changed in recent years because the numbers of unemployed people has fallen radically.

---

[6] Office of National Statistics (2005) 'Households below average income 1994/5–2003/4', Table 7.5; P. Spicker (2011) *How social security works*, Bristol: The Policy Press, p 255.

[7] J. Hills (2015) *Good times, bad times*, Bristol: The Policy Press, ch 4, p 107.

[8] From Department for Work and Pensions, continuing series, 'DWP tabulation tool', available at: https://www.gov.uk/government/collections/dwp-statistics-tabulation-tool

Table 2.1: Duration of claims

	All claimants	1 year or less	5 years or more
All	4,718,280	1,116,340	220,628
Job seekers	601,840	425,590	50,930
ESA and incapacity benefits	2,485,330	395,100	1,421,030
Lone parents	420,340	119,420	109,540
Carers	653,610	124,610	258,440
Others on income-related benefit	92,130	36,130	14,210

The figures in Table 2.1 show how many stick, not how many pass through the system. Over time, most claimants of working age claim for less than two years. About a fifth of working-age claimants are there for the very long term and about 90% of them receive incapacity benefits, which includes long-term chronic disability. There is very little evidence of longer-term dependency if that group is excluded – there are relatively few long-term claimants who are not incapacitated or caring for others. The position of carers reflects the position of people with disabilities. Most lone parents cease to be lone parents either because they find a partner or because their youngest child grows up. Long-term dependency on JSA is rare. The numbers of people unemployed for five years or more has increased in recent years, which probably reflects the reclassification of some people with long-term illnesses as unemployed, but they still account for only one jobless claimant in twelve. There is no support in these figures, then, for the idea that people are being trapped in long-term dependency by choice.

That does not mean, however, that no one is dependent. There is another very large group of people who do rely heavily on state benefits; benefits do support their lifestyle and they do not expect to work. They are called 'pensioners', and there are nearly 13 million of them, more if dependants, former public servants and expatriates are included. The difference is that their long-term dependency is generally thought to be legitimate, while the relatively short-term dependency of people of working age is not.

Disincentives to work

That leads fairly directly to the third part of the story: that the benefit system creates disincentives to work. Research for the Trades Union Congress (TUC) in 2013 found that:

> On average people think that an unemployed couple with two school-age children would get £147 in Jobseeker's Allowance – more than 30 per cent higher than the £111.45 they would actually receive.... Only 21 per cent of people think that this family with two school-age children would be better off if one of the unemployed parents got a 30 hour a week minimum wage job, even though they would actually end up £138 a week better off. Even those who thought they would be better off only thought on average they would gain by £59.[9]

It is not common for the position to arise that a person has a lower income in full-time work than on benefit. Benefits are very low relative to wages, and several benefits (including Child Benefit, Tax Credits, Housing Benefit and disability benefits) continue to be available while a person is working – a point often forgotten when people make comparisons between income from benefits and earnings. What may happen is that a person is not very much better off while working, because some of these benefits (Tax Credits and Housing Benefit) reduce when income increases. For a long time, Jobcentre Plus offered in-work calculations to show claimants that they would be better off, but doing the sums proved to be much less persuasive than governments had expected, and now they just direct claimants to online calculators. The problem is that in a 'flexible' labour market – or an insecure one – people are not sure what their position will really be

[9] Trades Union Congress (2013) 'Support for benefit cuts dependent on ignorance, TUC-commissioned poll finds', available at: https://www.tuc.org.uk/social-issues/child-poverty/welfare-and-benefits/tax-credits/support-benefit-cuts-dependent

like: whether the change in circumstances will undermine the security of their income, whether they will hold the job, whether they will get the amount of work they need and so on. The calculation says, 'here is how much money you will get', but the claimant might reasonably want to know, 'what is going to happen to me?', and the monetary figure is only a part of that. The Universal Credit scheme combines a fearsome 'marginal rate of deduction' – withdrawing benefits as income increases – with considerable uncertainty about how much will actually be paid month by month. It could have been expected to make the position far worse as it was first designed; subsequent revisions to the 'work allowance', how much someone could earn before deductions start, make it very questionable whether people will find it worthwhile to remain in contact with the benefit after they start work.

The arguments in the UK about incentives and disincentives are rather strange, because as they are framed they have little to do with motivation, or financial gain, or behaviour change or anything else that might be recognised as being about 'incentives'.[10] If the question is whether people are better or worse off if they become unemployed and claim benefits, the answer is overwhelmingly that they are worse off: the very low replacement ratios mean that it is unusual for people not to be. If the discussion was really about incentives, then there are some obvious ways to make sure that people are better off when working: fix their benefit according to their wages, put their wages up and get rid of some barriers to working like child care. What the debate in Britain does, however, is to take 'incentives' to mean something quite different: whether anyone on benefit, anywhere, is better off than the lowest paid worker, anywhere. This is fairly certain to happen, because anyone with high housing costs in one area will

[10] See P. Spicker (2006) 'Understanding incentives', in M. Steele (ed) *Report on incentive structures of social assistance grants in South Africa*, South Africa: Republic of South Africa Department of Social Development, available at: http://www.spicker.uk/open-access/2006%20Understanding%20 incentives.pdf

have a greater income from benefits than someone who lives in an area where housing costs are low.

The origins of the complaint that people are 'better off on the dole' run back to the days of the Poor Law. David Ricardo formalised the argument in an 'iron law of wages', which supposed that wages would always tend to be at the minimum level that a person needed to live, and that benefits might undercut those wages. The Poor Law Report of 1834 laid down a principle of 'less eligibility': that the situation of the pauper should always be 'less eligible', or less of an option, than the situation of the independent labourer. The situation of labourers was so bad that it was exceedingly difficult for the overseers of workhouses to make them any worse, and there were constant accusations that workhouses had become 'pauper palaces', where people could expect to be fed, clothed and sheltered when others could not be. The argument for 'incentives' is often little more than the argument for less eligibility, dressed in a different cardigan. It does not have much more to do with actual patterns of behaviour than the arguments about the Poor Law did. What it is really about is fairness: many people, especially those who work for low wages, do not think it fair that unemployed people should ever get more than employed people do.

Families where generations have never worked

There has been a resurgence of interest in families where no one has worked for generations. Louise Casey's report for the government was set up to examine 'entrenched cycles of suffering problems and causing problems'. She claimed that 'problems such as sexual abuse, teenage pregnancies, domestic violence, juvenile delinquency and educational failure were often repeated by different generations'.[11] Subsequently, the government has devoted its attention and resources

---

[11] L. Casey (2012) 'Listening to troubled families', Department of Communities and Local Government, available at: http://www.communities.gov.uk/documents/communities/pdf/2183663.pdf

to turning around the lives of 'troubled families', but the programme has had little effect.[12]

This argument has a long history. 'Troubled families' have been called 'degenerates', 'moral defectives', the 'abyss', 'problem families', 'multi-problem families', the 'hard to reach', the 'underclass' and much more.[13] The claim that they passed problems from one generation to another features in arguments on degeneracy, the culture of poverty, the cycle of deprivation, transmitted deprivation and the dependency culture. And what can be said about all of these arguments, because there are decades of evidence to draw on, is that they are not true. One of the leading studies in the 1970s was set up to examine 50 such families in depth; they could not find any, and had to settle for four who did not really fit the criteria.[14] For the most recent report on the subject, done for the Joseph Rowntree Foundation, the researchers searched 'doggedly' in areas of high unemployment for any family that had been deprived over the generations, and there wasn't anyone. They compared their search to the hunt for the Yeti.[15] The reasons for this are not difficult to explain. Most people in deprived circumstances will experience changes in those circumstances.[16] Most children from

[12] H. Bewley, A. George, C. Rienzo and J. Portes (2016) *National Evaluation of the Troubled Families Programme*, London: Department of Communities and Local Government, http://www.niesr.ac.uk/sites/default/files/publications/Troubled_Families_Evaluation_National_Impact_Study.pdf

[13] D. Matza (1967) 'The disreputable poor', in R. Bendix and S.M. Lipset, *Class status and power*, London: Routledge and Kegan Paul.

[14] F. Coffield and J. Sarsby (1980) *A cycle of deprivation?*, London: Heinemann.

[15] R. MacDonald, T. Shildrick and A. Furlong (2013) 'In search of intergenerational cultures of worklessness', *Critical Social Policy*, vol 34, no 2, pp 289–90.

[16] P. Buhr and S. Leibfried (1995) 'What a difference a day makes', in G. Room (ed) *Beyond the threshold*, Bristol: The Policy Press; R. Walker (1994) *Poverty dynamics*, Aldershot: Avebury; C. Heady (1997) 'Labour market transitions and social exclusion', *Journal of European Social Policy*, vol 7, no 2, pp 119–28.

deprived backgrounds are not deprived as adults.[17] Most adults have varying experiences through their lifetimes, and most will have spells on low income. In one key study, a thousand deprived families in Newcastle were followed through the generations. At every stage, the effect of economic change, education and partnering led to differences between parent and child, so that by the third or fourth generation the families in the cohort were indistinguishable from anyone else.[18]

Benefits for migrants

The debates about migrants and 'benefit tourism' have been crude, and at times toxic. The image projected in the press has been that the UK is a 'soft touch',[19] and that migrants are attracted to Britain by its generous and free-handed benefits system.[20] The repeated accusation that immigrants are drawn to Britain by the benefits system is baffling both to people who work with benefits and to those who engage with migrants. Part of the issue is that, as a simple matter of fact, most migrants come to Britain to work or to study. The other part is that the rules governing benefits for people coming into the UK are very

---

[17] A. Atkinson, A. Maynard and C. Trinder (1983) *Parents and children*, London: Heinemann.

[18] I. Kolvin, F.J.W. Miller, D.M. Scott, S.R.M. Gatzanis and M. Fleeting (1990) *Continuities of deprivation? The Newcastle 1000 family study*, Aldershot: Avebury.

[19] For example, P. Johnson (2001) 'Why is Britain regarded as a such a soft touch to the rest of the world?', *Daily Telegraph*, 19 May; T. Kelly (2012) 'Soft-touch Britain, the asylum seeker capital of Europe', *Daily Mail*, 29 June; A. Dawar (2014) 'EU migrants flock to "soft touch" Britain', *Daily Express*, 3 April.

[20] B. Waterfield (2014) 'Britain "too generous" with welfare payments to EU immigrants', *Telegraph*, 5 December; *Spectator* (2016) 'Whether or not Britain leaves, the EU must change or fall apart: generous welfare policies and open borders inevitably end in a nasty collision', 20 February; *Daily Express* (2016) 'How to get "GENEROUS" British benefits: shocking guide handed to Polish migrants', 10 March.

restrictive, and people who need to claim, especially shortly after they come to Britain, receive only limited help.

There may be some confusion because there are different types of in-migration, which are liable to be lumped together. Counts of 'net migration' are based on the numbers of people entering and leaving the country; that figure means very little as it stands. Many of those entering and leaving are visitors; more than 430,000 are students. 'Immigrants', properly speaking, are people who are aiming to settle – to live, work or raise a family. There are four main groups.

The first group consists of people and families from the European Economic Area (EEA) and the European Union, who, at the time of writing, still have the right to live and work in the UK. They may be entitled to benefits – the rules depend on the type of benefit, and, in several cases, there is some initial delay – but they are not particularly likely to claim them. The numbers of EEA migrants rose between 2014 from 5.6% of the workforce to 6.5%. The proportion claiming out-of-work benefits fell from 2.5% to 2.2.%. A higher proportion – 6.9% – received tax credits, which subsidise low wages.[21] In the longer term, these figures tend to balance out, so that a similar proportion of EEA nationals and UK citizens – 32% of EEA nationals, and 35% of UK nationals – get benefits of any kind.[22] However, people who are newly arrived from the EEA are much less likely to receive benefits.

The second category comprises other 'economic migrants', people and families who come to work from outside the EEA and who need permission to come to the UK. Many people within this category have been placed under restrictions, which mean that dependency on 'public funds' (including access to public housing, subsidised or not) will lead to termination of their stay. Despite that, those born outside the EEA are as likely to claim benefits as those from within it, and

---

[21] Migration Observatory (2016) *EU migration, welfare benefits and EU membership*, Oxford: University of Oxford, pp 6–7.

[22] Migration Observatory (2016) *EU migration, welfare benefits and EU membership*, Oxford: University of Oxford, p 10.

because their age profile also means that they are more likely to have children, they receive more in Child Benefit.[23]

The third category are people who come to join families living in the UK. Figures for this group have fallen from a peak of 74,000 in 2006 to a little over 50,000 in 2014, or about a fifth of non-EEA immigration.[24] They are also generally prevented from using public funds.

The fourth category are refugees and asylum seekers. The numbers are limited – just under 25,000 in 2015, and more than half the applications are ultimately rejected – but they are subject to a very different regime from other migrants. They are usually barred from working in the UK while their application is processed, and they have to depend on the special benefits systems made available for them.

The attention paid to migrants in the benefits system is disproportionate to their situation, to the costs or to the likelihood that they will receive help. In this, as in some other discussions of benefits, it does not seem to matter what is really happening. The indignation expressed by the press (and by some of the voices heard during the referendum to leave the European Union) seems to be not because the benefits are paid wrongly or unreasonably, but that they are paid at all. That may reflect a feeling that people should contribute before they are able to benefit, but it may equally represent a view that solidarity and social responsibility depend on issues of membership and identity.

Fraud and abuse

Among the long-running tropes in criticisms of social security, there is a consistent belief that lots of social security is claimed fraudulently. Prosecutions for fraud have featured extensively in the press since at least the 1970s. In the 1980s and 1990s, figures about fraud were

---

[23] Migration Observatory (2016) *EU migration, welfare benefits and EU membership*, Oxford: University of Oxford, p 10.

[24] See: http://www.migrationobservatory.ox.ac.uk/briefings/non-european-migration-uk-family-unification-dependents

more or less made up: Reg Prentice, the responsible minister in the early 1980s, had assumed that the estimates that were accepted for supermarkets about shoplifting would apply to social security as well.[25] The Green Paper published by the Labour government in 1997 accepted Prentice's rough guess as proven fact, and then added all the material they had some evidence for.[26] The hysteria has quietened down a little since, and current figures are based on sounder evidence. It helps to bear in mind that most benefits go to pensioners, and while there is some small amount of pensioner fraud (entitlement to most pensions has nothing to do with work, extra income or domestic lifestyle), the image of pensioners as fraudulent malingerers has never taken hold. Currently, the total losses through error and fraud in benefits administered by the Department for Work and Pensions (DWP) are estimated at £3.4 billion, while for Tax Credits and Child Benefit, the estimate is £2.3 billion. Note, however, that those figures are for error as well as fraud, and that error accounts for a good two-thirds of the total. The latest estimates are that 3.2% of claims featured error by claimants, 0.6% error by officials and 1.9% fraud. Three factors together – earnings and employment while claiming, income from occupational and personal pensions, and 'living together' or cohabitation – make up 44% of all the losses through fraud and error. This figure is less than many people expect, but when half the cost of the benefit system is down to relatively straightforward claims for State Pension or Child Benefit, the scope for fraud and error reduces.

Facts about social security are not difficult to find, but misunderstandings are rife. Frances O'Grady, the head of the TUC, sums up the misconceptions in these terms:

> It is not surprising that voters want to get tough on welfare. They think the system is much more generous than it is in reality,

---

[25] *Hansard* (1980) HC Deb.981-1156, 25 March.

[26] Department of Social Security (1998) *Beating fraud is everyone's business*, Cm 4012, London: Department of Social Security.

is riddled with fraud and is heavily skewed towards helping the unemployed, who they think are far more likely to stay on the dole than is actually the case. Indeed if what the average voter thinks was true, I'd want tough action too.

But you should not conduct policy, particularly when it hits some of the most vulnerable people in society, on the basis of prejudice and ignorance.... The truth remains that benefits are far from generous, the vast majority of the jobless are desperate for work and most benefit spending goes either on pensions or on benefits for those in jobs or who aren't able to work.[27]

[27] Trades Union Congress (2013) 'Support for benefit cuts dependent on ignorance, TUC-commissioned poll finds', available at: https://www.tuc.org.uk/social-issues/child-poverty/welfare-and-benefits/tax-credits/support-benefit-cuts-dependent

THREE

The real problems

The main task of this book so far has been to clear the ground – to challenge misconceptions about benefits. There are many real problems with the benefits system, but they are not the problems one hears most about.

The size of the operation

The first, and in some ways the most obvious, problem of the benefits system hardly gets mentioned in the critical coverage: that it is very big. It deals with millions of people in complex, highly diverse circumstances:

- more than 6 million people get means-tested, income replacement benefits (3.7 million of those are pensioners);
- more than 5 million people get help with housing costs;
- nearly 6 million people get help with paying council tax, mainly administered in local schemes; and
- there are nearly 13 million people in receipt of State Pension – one pound a week on the State Pension costs more than £670 million in a year.

The size alone has startling implications. There is a famous rule in engineering called Murphy's Law, telling us that 'anything that can go wrong will go wrong'. This is far from being a joke, even if it sounds like one. Any operation that goes through millions of iterations will have its weaknesses found out. It is useful to think in the same terms about social security. Whatever situation one could imagine, there are so many people in the system, and so many complexities in the circumstances that benefits deal with, that unlikely things are not just possible, but almost certain to happen. This comment comes from Lord Freud, a social security minister, who explained to the House of Commons Work and Pensions Committee how the pilot schemes for Universal Credit – still largely confined to jobless single people, at the time managing only a few thousand claims from over eight million initially expected – had shed a light on case management. He cited a 'rather complicated' case:

> Just to take an example of one of the more complicated cases we have had, we had a claimant who met a partner who had a son; they wanted to move in together and they therefore needed to move house and he had his own son moving in with them over the weekends. The new partner was in receipt of income support. What we got out of that rather complicated example was a partner claim, a child, a termination of tax credit, a termination of income support and a change of address. We were able to work that through, in policy terms, on a manual basis to find out how all those systems work.[1]

This example raises several troubling issues. One is that the system has clearly not been designed to take into account inconvenient changes in people's lives. New household formation is being treated as if it was exceptional, when it is commonplace. The assumption has been

[1] House of Commons Work and Pensions Committee (2013) 9 December, available at: http://data.parliament.uk/writtenevidence/WrittenEvidence. svc/EvidenceHtml/4338

made that people fall into a defined category, which then has to be modified. Second, half the 'problems' Freud is identifying seem to relate to the transition to Universal Credit itself. If that is right, this is a fundamental design fault likely to be experienced by millions of claimants. Third, at the stage when these comments were made, the development of Universal Credit had been going on for more than three years, and it seems that it was still unable to process a change in circumstances without managing it on a 'manual basis' – because, in other words, the system had not been designed to cope.

The human factor

Benefits are for people, and people do not always live in the way that governments want or expect them to do. People who receive benefits have choices to make. Part of the architecture of benefits is based on the idea that claims are 'subjective' – it is up to the claimant to make them. In the literature on social care, this is increasingly being referred to as 'co-production': the claimant has a role, as much as the service does.[2] Nothing can really work unless claimants take the initiative. (It does not have to be this way. People are not given a choice about whether or not they pay their taxes. There have been experiments with pensioners to show that the same can be done for the payment of benefits.[3] That, of course, is still subject to the general rule that things can and will go wrong; people will make of the evidence for and against what they choose to make of it.)

Much of the economic analysis of benefits depends on people being 'rational', at least to the degree that they do what is in their interests, or what right-wing political writers imagine is in their interests.[4]

[2] S. Osborne, Z. Radnor and G. Nasi (2013) 'A new theory for public service management?', *American Review of Public Administration*, vol 43, no 2, pp 135–58.

[3] L. Radford (2012) Quantitative evaluation of the Pension Credit Payment Study, London: DWP, https://www.gov.uk/government/uploads/system/uploads/attachment_data/file/214583/rrep796.pdf

[4] For example, C. Murray (1984) *Losing ground*, New York, NY: Basic Books.

It may be true that some people respond to incentives – there is some circularity in the idea, because if they do not it is not really an incentive – but it is not always clear what is an incentive, and what is not. The Department for Work and Pensions (DWP) is currently arguing that reducing benefits should act as a spur to those involved to find work; an independent research study suggests that it has the opposite effect, and claimants have to spend more time on day-to-day household management.[5] Some of the options that may seem to be 'rational' to commentators[6] are not what claimants choose to do. People do not claim money just because it is there. They do not unfailingly choose leisure before work. People of working age do not live on benefits in the long term if they have any way out. That is true partly because benefits do not actually work in the way that many of those commentators imagine – as Atkinson points out, there has never been a system that is unconditional and delivered uncritically.[7] It is no less true because people whose income is largely made up of benefits are generally much worse off than other people, despite the myths, and there is not much about their situation that could have the imagined effects.

It is more true that some of the routes people take may be predictable. People do what they have to do to survive. In the 1840s, Edwin Chadwick reported that people were getting help from the Poor Law because they were sick, not just because they were poor. By the time Beveridge wrote his report in the 1940s, every administrator knew that it was not possible to separate income support for unemployment and sickness: if there is no unemployment provision, people have to present as sick, and if there is no sickness provision, they have to present as unemployed. That is why Beveridge thought that it was necessary for there to be a National Health Service so that his unemployment

---

[5] P. Butler (2016) 'Docking benefits is not incentive to work, report claims', *Guardian*, 5 June.

[6] Such as C. Murray (1984) *Losing ground*, New York, NY: Basic Books.

[7] A. Atkinson (1990) *Institutional features of unemployment insurance and the working of the labour market*, London: Suntory-Toyota Centre for Economics and Related Disciplines.

insurance could work.[8] In the same way, provision for disability overlaps with provision for sickness: if there is no disability benefit, as there was not before the 1970s, people have to claim sickness benefits, and if there is no sickness benefit, people may have to claim disability benefits instead. This implies that it is at least possible to predict broad, aggregated trends – even if it tells us little about what any individual claimant will do in the circumstances.

Presumptuous administration

The complexity and variability of individual responses leads to a third major problem of the benefits system. Time and again, benefits have been designed on the basis that the agency operating the system will be able to process huge amounts of data to respond sensitively and flexibly to the changing circumstances of millions of people. Time and again, this approach has failed. When the Housing Benefit scheme was introduced in the early 1980s, the problem was not just that the authorities were being asked to work out benefits with two complicated formulas; it was that the local authorities needed to know about the house, the household composition and the income of thousands of families. The result was chaotic – it was called, in its day, 'the greatest administrative fiasco in the history of the welfare state'.[9] Some local authorities had not worked out benefits years after it was introduced, and had to keep making temporary payments on account while they caught up. Then there was the Child Support Agency, set up to make sure that absent parents paid for children from their former relationships. That often meant that an assessment needed to know the income, liability and household composition of two families – keeping track of six elements. Predictably, the administration proved

---

[8] Cmd. 6404 (1942) *Social insurance and allied services*, London: HMSO.
[9] *The Times*, cited in R. Walker (1986) 'Aspects of administration', in P. Kemp (ed) *The future of housing benefits*, Glasgow: Centre for Housing Research, p 39.

to be impossible – not for everyone, just for enough people to turn it into an unholy mess. There were simply too many moving parts.

The capacity of information technology to resolve this sort of issue has been oversold, nowhere more visibly than in the shambles that is Universal Credit – the leading minister was said to be 'hypnotised by promises of what an online system can deliver'.[10] There are limits to what computers can do, and a comprehensive system of benefit administration goes beyond them. Fifty years ago, Richard Titmuss berated the naivety of commentators who were convinced that computers could provide the answer to everything. He thought it absurd to expect a computer 'to solve the problems which human beings have not yet adequately diagnosed'. He pointed to the complexity of family lives, the lack of common characteristics, and the particular difficulties of applying general rules to the working-age population. He noted the problems that employers would have in collating information, especially information beyond the workplace, and the difficulty of coordinating benefits and tax. Above all, he emphasised that the rules and principles governing benefits called for issues of 'moral values, incentives and equity' to be taken into account. 'Computers', he wrote, 'cannot answer these questions'.[11]

The presumption goes deeper, however, than simply asking people for more information than the agencies know how to handle. There is a widespread assumption that all one has to do is to ask people the right questions, or get them to go through proper tests, and the answers will become clear. When Incapacity Benefit was introduced in the 1990s, it was assumed that a clearer, firmer definition of incapacity would make it possible to administer the benefit more strictly. The numbers of claimants fell a little at first, then returned stubbornly to where they had been before. So, the assessment process – the 'Personal Capacity Assessment' – was reformed into a more focused

[10] J. Cusick (2012) 'Benefits reform under threat after IT glitch', *Independent*, 11 November.

[11] R. Titmuss (1968) *Universal and selective social services, in Commitment to Welfare*, London: Allen and Unwin.

'Work Capability Assessment', and claimants were required to undergo personal assessments, and then to undergo further assessments at recurring intervals. There were hundreds of thousands of appeals, and about 40% of those heard were successful – which implies that many of the decisions were just plain wrong. (Unfortunately, there is no final figure – many of the appeals have disappeared in the Bermuda Triangle of benefits administration.) The main substance of the complaints, monitored in a series of independent reports, is that personal statements and medical evidence were ignored or dismissed.[12] The government has conceded at least that people with long-term conditions will not in the future be required to submit to repeated assessments. A similar process is also taking place to assess people for Personal Independence Payment (PIP), but while medical evidence is formally accepted, some of the same problems are still evident. Assessing people in this way is difficult, intrusive and inconvenient, and assessing millions of people is all of those things in large numbers, but that is not all of the problem. The sorts of questions that are being asked are the sorts of questions that people find it enormously difficult to answer. Most people who are disabled do not think that they are disabled. Others answer that they are disabled 'sometimes'.[13]

The same uncertainty and confusion is evident in claimants' position about their personal relationships and employment. Those readers who have gone through a divorce should be able to recognise the difficulty of saying for certain that a partner has gone, or that a new relationship is forming. Employment is also uncertain: for lower-paid employees, contracts of employment have become harder to obtain; people on zero-hours contracts do not know whether they have work until they do it; some employers insist (very questionably) on treating their employees as 'self-employed' in order to avoid having to meet

---

[12] For example, M. Harrington (2013) *An independent review of the work capability assessment – year 3*, London: HMSO, p 48.

[13] DWP, ad hoc analysis, Tables 10-11, available at: https://www.gov.uk/government/uploads/system/uploads/attachment_data/file/210030/q1-2013-data.xls

their statutory requirements; and pay can be unpredictable. The benefit system expects people to be able to say what they are doing and how it fits into the rules. Something that every benefits adviser must have heard is 'I don't know how to answer – tell me what I should say'. But when the claimants get it wrong, it is liable to be treated as fraud and harshly dealt with.

This raises serious doubts about one of the main objectives of contemporary policy, the plea for 'personalisation'. In theory, benefits ought to be able to respond to individual circumstances with sensitivity and precision. In practice, the more sensitive the requirements, the more difficult it is for the benefits to identify and respond appropriately: that is why highly individualised benefits like Pension Credit or PIP have such poor records for accuracy, while impersonal benefits such as the State Pension or Child Benefit work far better.

Conditionality

Joel Handler comments: 'Where morality is at issue, welfare is conditioned, regardless of any notional entitlement'.[14] It should not be surprising that politicians think that moral judgements have a place in delivering social security – a shared sense of moral responsibility is one of the key motivations for delivering social security in the first place. Regardless of the practical obstacles, the systems that are chosen or the rules that apply, social security is almost always subject to moral judgements.

The imposition of these judgements is most obvious in the treatment of people who are unemployed. There have been conditions of one sort or another for over a century that are intended to prevent 'moral hazard' – people making themselves entitled by making bad choices. A person who is unemployed 'voluntarily' or through misconduct could have benefits suspended. This is generally determined administratively by consulting the employer, for whom offences such as joining a trade union or failing to follow orders might well be considered misconduct.

[14] J. Handler (1972) *Reforming the poor*, New York, NY: Basic Books, p 24.

More recently, 'sanctions' or punishments have been extended for all kinds of infringements of the requirements of the benefits agency – failing to follow instructions, to appear for meetings at a set time or to be available when the jobcentre calls. The sanction can be imposed for four weeks, three months, six months or three years. Benefit sanctions, David Webster has written, have become 'a huge secret penal system, rivalling in its severity the mainstream judicial system but without the latter's safeguards'.[15] There have been hundreds of thousands of sanctions, affecting nearly a quarter of all jobseekers in the course of the last five years. The first findings from a large research project have reported that:

> The impacts of benefit sanctions are universally reported by welfare service users as profoundly negative. Routinely, sanctions had severely detrimental financial, material, emotional and health impacts on those subject to them. There was evidence of certain individuals disengaging from services or being pushed toward 'survival crime'. Harsh, disproportionate or inappropriate sanctioning created deep resentment and feelings of injustice among welfare service users.[16]

The demand for moral conduct sometimes seems to be common throughout the benefits system, but the situation is not as straightforward as it may seem. The 'cohabitation' rule tests whether people are living together as man and wife. The rationale for this is not directly judgemental. It is that a married couple receive less in benefits than two single people – or, say, two sisters, or a mother living with her adult son. It follows that wherever a couple might be treated as a couple, but claim separately, they are receiving more money than they

[15] D. Webster (2014) 'Evidence submitted (Dec 2014) to the House of Commons Work and Pensions Committee inquiry into benefit sanctions policy beyond the Oakley review', available at: http://www.cpag.org.uk/sites/default/files/uploads/CPAG-HofC-Wk-Pens-Sanctions-DW-evidence-Dec-2014.pdf

[16] P. Dwyer and J. Bright (2016) 'First wave findings: overview', available at: http://www.welfareconditionality.ac.uk/wp-content/uploads/2016/05/WelCond-findings-Overview-May16.pdf

are entitled to. There is a problem, then, in dealing with people fairly, which could only be settled otherwise if every claimant was treated as an individual. Unfortunately, the material difference between a couple and two sisters living in the same household boils down to something that benefits administrators cannot ask about, that is, sex. So, 'living together' is tested by a series of criteria – general relationship, social acknowledgement, children, shared meals together and so forth – when what the agency actually needs to know is whether people sleep with each other. Couples might be put under surveillance to discover the awful truth. For example, in September 2015, a Glasgow mother, Debbie Balandis, was challenged by Her Majesty's Revenue and Customs (HMRC) to explain her relationship with Martin McColl, a name they had discovered by examining Ms Balandis's financial transactions. Martin McColl is the trading name of RS McColl, a leading Scottish newsagent that also operates post offices. HMRC subsequently refused to admit its mistake and demanded evidence of the personal relationship.[17] Leave that intransigence aside for the moment: there is a serious issue lurking behind the silliness. What the agency had been doing was the kind of intrusive investigation that has been used to frustrate organised crime and terrorism, all in the hope of finding out whether a woman had been engaged in a relationship outside the bounds of marriage.

This is a small illustration of a much larger problem. HMRC had identified 1.5 million cases where they had concerns; they engaged Concentrix, a private firm, to process cases. Concentrix was reported to have sent out a million letters fishing for information, challenging for example whether they were not living with an undeclared partner;[18] the firm's representative told the House of Commons Work and Pensions Committee that they had sent out 324,000, though

---

[17] *Daily Record* (2015) 'Single mum has benefits stopped after HMRC accuse her of having relationship with local RS McColl branch', 30 September, available at: http://www.dailyrecord.co.uk/news/scottish-news/single-mum-benefits-stopped-after-6543039

[18] J. Stone (2016) 'Concentrix sent out a million spam letters fishing for tax credit errors, figures show', *Independent*, 15 September.

over a shorter period.[19] People who did not reply to the letters had their benefits stopped; a substantial majority of those who asked for reconsideration had the decision overturned. Frank Field MP, the Chair of the Committee, commented:

> The Committee was astonished by the extraordinary evidence we heard. From Concentrix we saw a company desperately out of their depth and unable to deliver on the contract awarded to them by HMRC. From senior HMRC officials we saw a palpable disregard for the human implications of this gross failure of public service. From the tax credit claimants we saw dignity in the face of appalling and traumatic experiences.[20]

There is a more general problem here than the failure of a particular contract. There are limits to what benefits agencies can hope to know, and the information needed to enforce these rules went far beyond the capacity of the administration. This is something that benefits systems cannot hope to do fairly and effectively.

Complexity

It should not be surprising that benefits systems are complex; they need to be. They have multiple aims, they deal with a huge range of different conditions and circumstances, and they deal with complex lives. What seems to happen next, however, is that politicians respond to the problems by making the situation more complex still. Recent examples include:

[19] House of Commons Work and Pensions Committee (2016) 'Proceedings', 13 October, available at: http://www.parliamentlive.tv/Event/Index/c7a299f0-96ca-436e-9e30-81216274cdeb

[20] A. Cowburn (2016) 'Disabled mother fights back tears recalling dealings with welfare contractor Concentrix', *Independent*, 14 October, available at: http://www.independent.co.uk/news/uk/politics/disabled-single-mother-fights-back-tears-recalling-dealings-with-welfare-contractor-concentrix-a7359766.html

- a limit to the amount of benefit that someone of working age can receive;
- clawing back Child Benefit from richer families;
- rules to make sure that families are not paid for spare bedrooms;
- special rules for single people to stop them getting bigger housing;
- rules to limit the rights of recent migrants to the UK; and
- restrictions on the age when young people can claim certain benefits.

Any of these rules could be criticised in its own right, but quite apart from that, each change pulls a clutch of new problems in its wake. The rules have to be clarified in order to explain who is being included in them and who is not. What is a spare bedroom? How long does someone have to live in the UK before they stop being a migrant? Which benefits get restricted, and which do not? Then, like most general rules, they do not work for everyone. So, at the same time that the government introduces the rules, it also has to introduce a range of exceptions – benefits that are not included in the benefit cap, classes of claimant who will be affected and others who will not, rooms that are not to be counted as accommodation, and so on. Currently, there are plans to suspend benefits for the third child in a family, unless the child is born as a result of rape. That exception means that there will have to be a rape test – some way of distinguishing women who have been raped from the rest.[21] The exception might be well-meaning, but it is hard to think of any way of implementing it that would not be intrusive, humiliating and deeply unpleasant. A further set of problems comes because any rules like this have to cope with the dizzying complexity of people's lives. Age is fairly predictable, but family composition can change rapidly, and income changes suddenly and sometimes catastrophically.

[21] H. Stewart and R. Mason (2016) 'UN asks government to explain two-child cap on child tax credits', *Guardian*, 21 May, available at: https://www.theguardian.com/society/2016/may/21/two-child-cap-child-benefit-un-snp

Complexity cannot be avoided altogether, because any rule to define who is entitled to benefit has to be interpreted somehow. There cannot be a benefit for sickness without there being some distinction between people who are sick and those who are not; if there is going to be an unemployment benefit, there has to be some way of determining whether someone is unemployed. Some of the complexities, then, are intrinsic to the benefits – they are part and parcel of what the benefits are supposed to do. However, there are also avoidable complexities, of two kinds.

First, there are rules that are just more convoluted than they need to be to do the job. (My apologies if the examples that follow are difficult to make sense of, but that is the point.)

- National Insurance entitlements for some benefits are based on contributions made one or two tax years (running April–March) preceding the immediate calendar year (running January–December).
- Actual income from capital is disregarded for means tests, but capital is means-tested on a nominal scale.
- Entitlement to rent is usually calculated on a weekly basis, but lots of social landlords have two rent-free weeks around Christmas time, so the non-dependent deductions and income are recalibrated, and rent is recalculated at 50/52 of the nominal level.
- Universal Credit is being paid on the same day of the month as the initial claim, a date which loses its significance as soon as someone gets their first pay cheque. It means that claimants can be paid on any one of 31 days, and that those days need to be shunted around for bank holidays and 30- or 28-day months.

Then, there are rules that are introduced deliberately to vary the terms on which the system works for others – trying to bar the wrong sort of person from claiming benefit, trying to remove barriers for others, trying to personalise the response. It is not that decision-makers actually say to themselves, 'the system is not complicated enough yet'; it is rather that they think they can stand a little more complexity to do the terribly important thing that they absolutely have to do this time around. Examples of the first type – trying to bar the wrong sort of claim – are the rules which say that people have to be looking actively for work for 35 hours a week (impossible to verify, but nevertheless one of the main grounds for benefits being withdrawn)[22]; that although strikers already cannot get benefit, strikers' families should also have elements deducted from their benefit entitlement; or that people who come to live in Britain should have to wait an extra period before they become entitled to disability benefits. Examples where the special rules have been supposed to encourage people to claim benefits might be the Savings Credit, an extra means test meant to allow pensioners on very low incomes to keep some income from savings which would otherwise be deducted from means-tested benefits, or the rules that allow older people receiving Disability Living Allowance (DLA) to get extensions into retirement age.

The administrative complications are fuelled by the assumption that if any general rule is introduced, everyone has to be checked individually. So, every claimant of Jobseekers Allowance (JSA) or Universal Credit has to sign a 'commitment' about looking for work; every claimant of Employment and Support Allowance (ESA) has to be assessed for their capacity to work; everyone has to be warned about the dire consequences of fraud; and every form must be signed. ESA refuses to accept basic evidence from medical practitioners who have given continuing care for patients over extended periods of time, or even from leading experts dealing with the medical condition. Not long after the process of reassessing ESA claimants had become the subject of extended delays, misjudgements and protests, and the firm commissioned to do the work had thrown in the towel, the government extended the same kind of process to PIP.

[22] D. Webster (2016) 'Explaining the rise and fall of JSA and ESA sanctions 2010-60', available at: http://www.cpag.org.uk/sites/default/files/uploads/16-08%20Supplement%20-%20Reasons%20for%20rise%20%20fall%203%20Oct%2016.docx

Correcting mistakes

It is inevitable that benefits agencies will make mistakes. The sheer numbers they deal with, the complexity of the people's circumstances and the uncertainty of the information they are dealing with all add to that; however, even if the system was perfect, things would go wrong. One of the central tests of any system, then, is how mistakes can be rectified. That is basic to treating service users properly. It is no less important for any agency to be able to learn from its mistakes – 'critical incidents', such as complaints, requests for review and appeals, can provide managers with essential information about how the schemes are really operating, and what needs to be done to improve them.

Thirty years ago, in the days of the Department of Health and Social Security, the benefit system was remarkable both for the speed of its decision-making and the slowness of rectification. The offices worked on strictly Fordist principles, as if they were a production line: cases went to stations in a 'stream'. If people had problems, the case papers had to be taken out of the stream, often leading to delays – first, in finding where the file had got to, and then in feeding back the case so that other issues could be reviewed. Revisions, internal reviews and appeals all extended the time it took to process decisions. The development of information technology should have made all this unnecessary: it should mean that cases can be reviewed and details revised electronically, simultaneously with every other process.

Instead, the process of review has become substantially more difficult. The first problem is in establishing contact to exchange information; the registration of online information, the closure of local offices and the increasingly restricted use of telephone contact makes it difficult to enlist the aid of a human being. In the new Universal Credit system, officials in Jobcentre Plus are not permitted to take or act on information from claimants, who have to be directed back to the online system if, for example, they move house or find work. The second problem lies in the obstacles to internal review: officials are not trusted to correct errors. It has long been true of the culture of the benefits system that those who operate at the centre complain that officials fail to comply with their instructions, while those who work in the offices have to find ways around the inadequacies of the same centralised systems to make them work. The tendency has been to put the onus of making corrections on claimants: the system of 'mandatory reconsideration' (MR) is mandatory on claimants, who have to go through the formal process of registering a claim for consideration. The Social Security Advisory Committee's report on MR identifies many of the problems with this process – for example, the need for claimants to put in multiple requests to cover a series of decisions. They undermine this, unfortunately, by the anodyne conclusion that MR 'could be an efficient process that provides opportunity for timely review'.[23] It could not be and it does not. The effect of mandating an additional process prior to any appeal does not act to increase official scrutiny (which took place before any appeal in the former system), but it does impose a barrier on claimants seeking redress. As this stage – actually a sequence of processes – is mandatory for claimants, there is a delay in correcting any error: barriers to access are obstacles to justice, and justice delayed is justice denied.

The third problem is the most fundamental. Decisions made against a claimant are implemented before any response or contrary case has been considered[24]: sentence first, verdict afterwards. The process of MR does not offer claimants the opportunity to know of and respond to information relating to their case. One of the central principles of administrative law is 'natural justice', and part of that is *audi alteram partem*, the principle that people must hear the arguments against themselves and have the opportunity to respond to them. Michael Adler argues that the system of benefit sanctions, and the subsequent failures of redress, fails to meet accepted standards for the rule of law on several grounds, including proportionality, the right to be heard, balance between parties and compliance with international law:

---

[23] Social Security Advisory Committee (2016) *Decision making and mandatory reconsideration*, London: SSAC.

[24] M. Adler (2016) 'A new Leviathan: benefit sanctions in the twenty-first century', *Journal of Law and Society*, vol 43, no 2, pp 195–227.

the combination of review/reconsideration and appeal procedures does not provide an adequate amount of procedural protection for those who are sanctioned and that, taking their severity, incidence, and impact into account, benefit sanctions are not only disproportionate but also inconsistent with justice.[25]

The limited access to redress is reinforced by another troubling legal decision. The main legal recourse is through tribunals, but their remit is limited. Judicial review of administrative action in the courts is expensive, complex, slow and only available when other recourse (including MR) has been exhausted. In the 1990s, the House of Lords (now the Supreme Court) accepted that it was too difficult for the benefits authorities to reprocess cases where decisions had been made through a mistake of law.[26] The 'anti-test case' rule means that legal decisions that show the department to have made mistakes should not lead to the retrospective correction of those mistakes. This seems to have been taken by ministers as a reason to fight decisions all the way, because that is the most effective way to minimise the general liabilities that acceptance of different rules would imply. The rule effectively means that, in most cases, there is no effective redress for past injustice, a situation that disgraces both the legal system and British public administration.

Selectivity

The core problem of complexity reflects the practice of 'selectivity'. Selectivity is sometimes confused with means-testing (of which more shortly), but it is a more general term than that. Usually, it implies the selection of people on the basis of means or need, so it would include not only tests of income, but also the sort of tests required of people with disabilities.

---

[25] M. Adler (2015) 'Benefit sanctions and the rule of law', available at: https://ukaji.org/2015/10/14/benefit-sanctions-and-the-rule-of-law/

[26] CAO and another v Bate, [1996] 2 All ER 790 (HL).

The first basic principle of selectivity is that a distinction has to be drawn between people who are eligible to receive the benefit and those who are not. To claim assistance with paying for a funeral, the process asks six things: the personal circumstances of the applicant, their financial resources, their relationship to the deceased person, the resources of the estate, the arrangements that have been made for the funeral and whether anyone else might be responsible for meeting the costs. There are 36 pages in the form, though, in fairness, the first 10 pages are explanatory notes (or administrative gobbledegook) rather than things that the applicant absolutely has to work through. The most difficult thing about filling in the form is probably not the means test, but the last part – explaining the family and personal relationships that lead to one person rather than another taking responsibility.

Almost all benefits define eligibility in some way. If the criterion for eligibility is straightforward membership of a category – for example, people over 80, pensioners' bus passes or benefits for children under 16 – there is no need to develop a process for exclusion. (These are real examples.) Income tax is not thought of as a selective process, because everyone is included until they can find a way to opt out; when we had means-tested student grants, those were not treated as selective either. The difference between selective benefits and others is the second part – the process of exclusion. Selection sorts out the sheep from the goats, and sometimes they can be hard to tell apart. So, there are tests to decide how sick or disabled people are, whether they are actively seeking work, how much money they have coming in, and so on. Often, the tests are poorly understood. A study of unsuccessful claims for DLA found that people receiving ESA – the long-term sickness benefit – did not understand that DLA was there for different purposes. They sometimes made claims with no reasonable hope of success, thinking that they may as well have a crack at it; if they were refused, they put it down to luck rather than the operation of appropriate criteria.[27] (The transition from DLA to PIP is being

[27] A. Thomas (2008) *Disability Living Allowance: Disallowed claims*, London: DWP.

done at a time of swingeing cuts in entitlement to ESA, and there seems to be very little prospect of undoing the muddle in the course of redefining the benefits.)

The language of 'selectivity' does not identify a straightforward category of benefits. There is a spectrum of eligibility conditions and tests, and the more stringent the tests, the more selective the benefit is. There is more selectivity for some benefits, such as ESA, than there is for others, such as Industrial Injuries Disablement Benefit. JSA is less selective for the first six months, when there is a contributory test, than it is later on. Child Benefit used to have hardly any selectivity, but the government recently introduced a mechanism through the tax system for excluding richer families.

The most basic argument for selectivity is that benefits need to be delivered to people in need. If benefits are meant to help those in need, there has to be some way of identifying who those people are. If there were no selection, there would be no practical way of responding to specific needs when they do arise. Some degree of selectivity is necessary in a benefits system; we could not provide for people with disabilities without it. Unfortunately, it is not possible to do this without some complexity, and the more finely tuned the rules are, the more problematic benefits become. There are always problems of inclusion, where people qualify for the benefit who are not in the target group, and exclusion, where people do not get the benefits they should. Benefits commonly fail to reach the people they are intended for. Most of the available figures focus on means-tested benefits, but there are the same kinds of problems with all selective benefits. Table 3.1 shows estimates, drawn from a range of sources.[28]

[28] DWP (2016) 'Income related benefits: estimates of takeup 2014/15', available at: https://www.gov.uk/government/statistics/income-related-benefits-estimates-of-take-up; HMRC (2016) 'Child Benefit, Child Tax Credit and Working Tax Credit: take-up rates 2013 to 2014', available at: https://www.gov.uk/government/statistics/child-benefit-child-tax-credit-and-working-tax-credit-take-up-rates-2013-to-2014; DWP (2012) 'Income related benefits: estimates of takeup 2009-10 (for Council Tax Benefit, precedessor of Council Tax Support)' London: DWP, https://www.gov.uk/

The outcomes for means-tested benefits are bad; the outcomes for disability benefits, which are not means-tested, are worse.

Table 3.1: The take-up of various benefits

	Type of benefit	Estimates of take-up by eligible recipients	Estimates of the amount of money due that is being claimed
Child Benefit	Universal	95–96%	–
Child Tax Credit	Tapered	85–89%	91–94%
Housing Benefit	Tapered	79%	86%
Income Support (and income-related ESA)	Minimum income	82%	84%
Working Tax Credit	Tapered	66–71%	84–87%
Pension Credit	Minimum income	62%	69%
Council Tax Support	Tapered	62–69%	64–71%
Jobseekers Allowance	Insurance/minimum income	50%	57%
Disability Living Allowance mobility component	Non-contributory	50–70%	–
Attendance Allowance	Non-contributory	40–60%	–
Disability Living Allowance care component	Non-contributory	30–50%	–

The other problems that are hard to avoid are the boundary problems – the difficulty of deciding where the boundary should fall, of who is in and who is out. This is often identified with the 'poverty trap' – withdrawing benefits gradually makes it uncertain when entitlement starts and when it finishes – but it is more complicated than that. In

government/uploads/system/uploads/attachment_data/file/222914/tkup_first_release_0910.pdf; D. Kasparova, A. Marsh and D. Wilkinson (2007) *The takeup rate of Disability Living Allowance and Attendance Allowance: Feasibility study*, London: Department for Work and Pensions.

Scotland, free personal care for elderly people is based on an assessment, and the assessment determines entitlement to support and provision. When free personal care was introduced, it seemed at first as though the demand was limited, and largely known. As the system has become established, the pressure on services – and their expense – has been growing. This is a common pattern with selective benefits. It happened with single payments, where highly restrictive entitlements for special needs were progressively tested through applications and appeals; with the assessment of incapacity, where a points system laying down strict criteria for qualification admitted increasing numbers of claims; and for DLA, where the initial rules were gradually bent to accommodate the needs of people with mental illness or fluctuating conditions. In all of those cases, politicians and administrators were convinced that all they needed to do was to tighten up the rules and the costs would fall. It rarely works that way. People claim what they can; if the distinction is a matter of fine judgement, some will be deterred and others will try to make sure that they can satisfy the requirements. These judgements cannot be made consistently, accurately and fairly, and inevitably attempts to personalise have to accept some degree of compromise.

Then there are problems of fraud and error. The popular conception here is that fraud is the main problem; the best evidence, outlined in Table 3.2,[29] suggests that the problem of error is much greater. The official statistics are sometimes questionable – HMRC claims to have made hardly any mistakes – and the figures for error are probably an underestimate, because the samples that it is based on are samples of claims; people who have been wrongly denied the benefit are not included in the figures.

---

[29] DWP (2016) 'Fraud and error in the benefit system', available at: https://www.gov.uk/government/uploads/system/uploads/attachment_data/file/528719/fraud-and-error-prelim-estimates-2015-16.pdf; HMRC (2015) 'Child and Working Tax Credits error and fraud statistics 2013 to 2014', available at: https://www.gov.uk/government/statistics/child-and-working-tax-credits-error-and-fraud-statistics-2013-to-2014

Table 3.2: Estimates of errors in the benefit system (percentages of value)

	Fraud	Claimant error	Official error	Total
JSA				
Overpaid	3.2	0.4	1.5	5.0
Underpaid	0.1	0.1	0.7	0.8
Pensions Credit				
Overpaid	2.5	1.4	1.7	5.6
Underpaid	0	0.7	1.6	2.3
Housing Benefit				
Overpaid	3	1.8	0.4	5.2
Underpaid	0	1.0	0.4	1.4
DLA				
Overpaid	0.5	0.6	0.8	1.9
Underpaid	0	2.4	0.1	2.5
State Pension				
Overpaid	0	0.1	0	0.1
Underpaid	0	0	0.2	0.2
ESA				
Overpaid	1.7	0.5	0.6	2.8
Underpaid	0	1.0	1.4	2.3
Universal Credit				
Overpaid	5.4	0.2	1.7	7.3
Underpaid	0	0.4	2.3	2.6
Tax credits				
Overpaid	2.4	2.9	0	5.3
Underpaid	no data	no data	no data	0.5

The figure for Pension Credit is noteworthy because it is the only figure that can be compared directly to an alternative method of payment, the State Pension. These benefits go to a very similar population, but State Pension is easy to claim and Pension Credit is convoluted. In relation to Pension Credit, overpayment through fraud stands at 1.8%, 'customer' error at 1.3% and official error at 1.5%, making 4.6% altogether. By contrast, the equivalent figures for State Pension are 0.0%, 0.1% and 0.0%, respectively. The message is clear: if benefits are to get to the right people, they need to be simpler.

Means testing

Means testing ought, on the face of the matter, to ensure that people on low incomes have their incomes supplemented without wasting resources on people who do not have the same needs. Economists often argue that systems that respond to the circumstances of individuals are more efficient than those that do not, and one of the primary arguments for means testing has always been that the benefits will be allocated more efficiently – spending less money to greater effect. Unfortunately, this is not how things work in practice. Many of the problems of means testing are the problems of selectivity. There are problems of policing the boundaries and of fairness; there are inevitably problems with imposing conditions, running tests, and excluding people. However, means testing also has problems of its own, partly due to the focus on financial resources, and partly to the processes that are needed to track them. The first problem is knowing where to draw the lines. The lower the income threshold, the higher the rate of withdrawal and the meaner the benefit will be. The shape of the distribution of income means that means-tested benefits are condemned to be either restrictive or very expensive.

The second problem is a problem of equity. Means testing is largely based on a test of financial resources, but not all resources are financial. In the past, there have been tests that required people to sell their possessions, but these have been extremely unpopular. That implies that some people will have carpets, cars or televisions and others will not. If the purpose of benefits is to smooth income, this is not a problem: the point of some benefits (like contributory JSA and ESA) is to fill in gaps so that people will not have to be suffer as a result of the interruption of their income. That is not true in this case: one of the main justifications for means testing is to relate income to resources, and the tests that are based solely on income and capital rely on a compromise.

Then there are the specific administrative problems of trying to track resources. They include:

- The problem of defining the threshold for entitlement – and the obvious unfairness that happens when some people are just above the qualifying level.
- The speed at which income changes – month to month, week to week, even day to day. The increasing reliance on 'flexible' labour markets mean that the income of lower-paid people fluctuates rapidly and unpredictable – a 'roller coaster'.
- The difficulty of treating saving fairly, because saving often depends on past income rather than present resources.
- The way that resources are shared in a household, and the ways in which people who live together in different arrangements are treated. Most of the non-means-tested benefits are only concerned with the person who is claiming. Means-tested benefits have to be concerned with other people around the claimant – another set of circumstances that is liable to rapid and unpredictable change.

Means testing has proved in practice to be, not the cheapest and most tightly circumscribed way of delivering a benefit, but the opposite. The benefits that have mushroomed unexpectedly since the 1970s – Supplementary Benefit and Income Support, Housing Benefit, and Tax Credits – are mainstream, means-tested benefits. They are complex, covering multiple contingencies, they are expensive to run, and they are riddled with administrative pitfalls, but none of that really sets means testing apart. The plain fact is that means tests have proved far more difficult to control and regulate than politicians (and theoretical economists) imagine. Entitlement to these benefits is based primarily on the fact that people have low incomes, and as very large numbers of people live on low incomes, there is not much that can effectively be done to deny them. In relation to each of these benefits:

- Governments imagined that they were dealing with a smaller set of issues than proved to be the case. Supplementary Benefit descended from National Assistance, which was supposed to wither away as more people became entitled to National Insurance; Housing

Benefit was supposed to fill the gaps for social renting while owner-occupation was expanding; and tax credits, for lower-paid workers, would cost £2 billion rather than the £30 billion they proved to cost.

- Policymakers thought that managing needs through the market would lead to greater allocative efficiency. Supplementary Benefit and Income Support were used – very effectively – to finance the private care sector; Housing Benefit was intended to move subsidies from housing to individual households; and Tax Credits have paid for childcare by giving people the money to spend, rather than providing places directly. In each case, this approach has led to costs mounting rapidly. (Something similar is likely to happen with the growth of independent budgets in social care.)

- Governments believed that if costs increased, they would be able to restrict them by tightening the criteria, and, in particular, that using a formula or threshold would target benefits and keep the costs down. The rules for Income Support tightened up Supplementary Benefit, reducing the scope for individuals to claim extras; the costs of single payments were to be held down by blocking claims to clothing; Housing Benefit saw progressive changes in its formulas, altering the thresholds and the tapers; the costs of Housing Benefit would be held down by tightening the local housing allowance or the bedroom tax; Tax Credits are being limited to two children and tapers have been hiked up, but the growing number of claims stems from changes in the labour market.

Insanity, Einstein famously suggested, is repeatedly doing the same thing in the belief that next time the results will be different. The design of Universal Credit, which is slowly being rolled out across the UK, brings together every major feature that has caused administrative meltdown in the course of the last forty years: personalisation, tapers, computerisation, conditionality and multiple moving parts. It is as if the designers had painstakingly identified all the elements of the benefit system that are known not to work and built the new benefit around them.

FOUR

How much is enough?

Cash and the private market

Although there are clearly going to be important differences in the aims and approaches of different benefits, there are two big things that are generally true of all of them. The first is that because they are paid as money, people get to use that money to buy things. There are many circumstances where people do not get cash, but receive a service instead. The National Health Service, the system of schools, roads and household rubbish collection are paid for by taxation, not by people paying fees, and they are organised so that people get the service rather than giving them money to buy the services. By contrast, there are other contingencies where people get benefits instead of getting the service. Working Tax Credit pays for childcare; if there was proper funding of public childcare, as there is in other countries, it might not have to be paid as a benefit. Housing Benefit pays for rent; it had to be introduced because of a decision to cut the general subsidy that was paying for council housing. The bill has been spiralling upwards, largely because social landlords have been forced to put up their rents.

It follows that it is not enough to say that people need to have something important – food, fuel, health care or schooling. It matters how their needs will be met – whether they should have money or whether the need is better met in some other way. If children do not get enough to eat, the family might receive more in benefits, or there might be free school meals. If older people cannot afford heating, they may get more money, or there may be measures to help them make their house warmer. In England, people of working age have to pay for medical prescriptions, and if they cannot afford them, they have to claim a benefit. In Scotland and Wales, prescriptions are provided free as part of the provision made by the health service.

Paying people money also assumes that they will be able to spend it, and that depends on the mechanisms of a private market. On the one hand, there is a broad consensus in the UK that health care is too important to be left to the market. On the other hand, there is an even stronger consensus, which is rarely questioned, that food ought to be bought, rather than supplied. After the Second World War, Britain had food rationing – the control of the production, distribution and marketing of key foodstuffs – but this was all phased out. If people are short of food, the way to deal with it is not to have a National Food Service, but for them to have the money to pay for food. One of the reasons for paying social security, to add to those in the list in Chapter One, is providing funding for the development of a private market. Another is to promote privatisation, because it is only really possible to steer provision back to the private market if poor people have the resources to get essential services. Free-marketeers such as Friedman and Seldon[1] generally hold that markets are a better way to provide goods to people than public services. If the main objection to privatising services is that some people will not be able to afford them, then the answer is to redistribute money, not to control the distribution of the service. So, there are cases where social security has been used deliberately, in preference to service provision, as a way of promoting the development of the private market; that has been true in the past of the provision of residential care and of Housing Benefit.

That seems to imply that people who are in favour of extending the role of markets really ought to be in favour of social security

---

[1] A. Seldon (1977) *Charge!*, London: Temple Smith; M. Friedman and R. Friedman (1981) *Free to choose*, Harmondsworth: Penguin.

benefits, and that the people who are against them ought to be against benefits. Often, the opposite applies. The right-wingers who argue for freedom, markets and private property also tend to be the ones who are most strongly opposed to granting people money to spend. By contrast, left-wing socialists and anti-capitalists are very likely to argue that benefits need to be protected and improved. What both positions have in common is a sense that social security is only ever a part of the story: it is a way of doing things, not the answer to every problem. Looking at social security, and nothing but social security, can never be enough.

Income packages

The second big thing to say about benefits is that money can be lumped together with other money. Once different sums of money are put together, there is not much distinction that can be made between them. Despite the assumption that people feel a sense of entitlement to insurance benefits that they do not feel for means-tested benefits, it is hard to imagine that older people really suppose that the money they get from their State Pension should be treated differently to the money they get from Pension Credit, and no survey evidence suggests that they do. The technical term for this is that money is 'fungible' – it can be mixed together. What really matters about benefits, some researchers have argued, is the 'income package': what people have when everything is put together.[2] There are occasions when the entitlement to one benefit reduces entitlement to others – some benefits are knocked off the value of means-tested benefits; the way that benefits are defined means that it is not possible to be treated as a carer and an unemployed person at the same time. On the whole, however, what will happen to a benefit is that it will be added to other benefits and other income. It follows, then, that every proposal to introduce a new benefit has to consider not just whether there is a

[2]   L. Rainwater, M. Rein and J. Schwartz (1986) *Income packaging in the welfare state*, Oxford: Oxford University Press.

reason to offer support, and not just whether it should take the form of cash, but another further question: how much difference will it make?

These are difficult issues. There was a time when state pensions were expected to be the only income that people would have in old age, so the level of benefit that had to be provided by the state pension had to be adequate to live on. This never worked as intended. Most countries have a three-tier pensions system, and Britain is no exception. In the first tier, there are people who have an occupational or private pension, usually going along with the National Insurance pension. Then there are people who have only a limited occupational or private pension, for whom the basic State Pension is central. The third tier consists of people who have no pension entitlement, or an inadequate entitlement, and they are supposed to get a guaranteed minimum income through a top-up benefit – this is now done in Britain through the Pension Credit. What, then, does an 'adequate' pension look like? There are three perfectly reasonable answers here – an earnings-related income, a basic income and a minimum income – which all lead in different directions. It is not difficult to think *why* there should be pensions. The main problems that need to be addressed are *how* pensions should be paid, and *how much* they should be.

How much should benefits be?

Recent governments have worked hard to give the impression that benefits in Britain are excessively generous. With its first attempt at the 'benefits cap', the government suggested that benefits might otherwise shell out more than £26,000 a year. It is possible, but the numbers of people of whom that might be true are tiny – the initial estimates suggested that there might be 80,000, then 55,000, then 40,000, then, as the real figures came through, 28,500. This is out of more than 7 million working-age claimants, not counting the receipt of Child Benefit. There are obvious questions as to how people might come to have such high benefits at all. It happens rarely; when it does, it usually reflects very high housing costs, either for rent or to meet mortgage interest. However, this is hardly a normal representation of the circumstances of benefits claimants. The basic rate of benefit is £181.65 for a pensioner couple (£9,445 a year) and £114.85 per week for an unemployed couple (£5,972 a year). That low figure is also what should be borne in mind when comparing the position of people on benefit to people in work. Housing Benefit will be available for those who rent – but the same benefit is available at a more generous rate for people who are working.

Far from being generous, the British system offers only mediocre support, which is particularly ungenerous to single people who are not renting their housing. Table 4.1 is drawn from a long series of data presented by the Organisation for Economic Cooperation and Development (OECD).[3] This table is based on average replacement ratios – that is, how much benefits offer by comparison with wages – over five years. Benefits in the UK start out lower than many benefits elsewhere, but they are not reduced for longer-term unemployment. Most unemployed people in the UK – still over 80% – are employed within a year, and (as Table 2.1 showed) very few are continuously unemployed and claiming benefits after five years, so this picture may be slightly flattering to the UK.

The Council of Europe, an intergovernmental organisation that monitors compliance with international agreements in human rights and social provision, has commented that:

> the situation in United Kingdom is not in conformity with Article 12§1 of the Charter on the grounds that:
> - the minimum level of short-term and long-term incapacity benefit is manifestly inadequate;
> - the minimum level of state pension is manifestly inadequate;
> - the minimum level of job seeker's allowance is manifestly inadequate.[4]

---

[3] See: http://www.oecd.org/els/benefits-and-wages-statistics.htm

[4] Council of Europe (2014) 'European Social Charter – European Committee of Social Rights – conclusions XX-2 (2013) Great Britain', Strasbourg: Council of Europe.

Table 4.1: Average of net replacement rates over 60 months of unemployment, 2014

	Claimant does not qualify for cash housing assistance or social assistance top-ups			Claimant qualifies for cash housing assistance or social assistance top-ups		
	Single person	Couple, one earner, 2 children	Overall average	Single person	Couple, one earner, 2 children	Overall average
Denmark	40	51	47	69	76	72
Netherlands	26	35	29	63	78	70
Switzerland	22	26	24	56	79	69
Japan	9	15	13	54	73	65
Belgium	62	64	64	62	64	64
Sweden	30	42	37	51	72	63
Germany	28	53	42	45	74	61
UK	17	52	32	46	75	61
France	44	46	45	53	65	59
Australia	27	61	48	33	63	52
Canada	11	38	25	32	67	52
USA	4	4	4	11	39	25
Italy	9	9	9	9	9	9

There is no unambiguous, universal standard of adequacy, nor could there be; the Council of Europe's judgement has been made by comparison with other countries. For several years, the European Union has used a relative standard of 'economic distance', now officially referred to as an indicator of being 'at risk' of poverty. This is an income of 60% of the median income, adjusted for household size and composition. This is rather a parsimonious test – the median income is rather less than the average wage, so the test compares people on very low incomes to others whose are not very adequate – and it is a measure of income inequality rather than need. The rationale for using it is that people's ability to obtain resources depends not only on what they have, but on what other people have – housing, the condition of local areas and the amenities that can be provided depend on the resources of the community, not on the individual. There is a degree of arbitrariness in using this test, made more arbitrary still when housing costs are left out of the calculation.

The next problem is to adapt this crude standard to take into account different sizes of household. Table 4.2 draws heavily on work by Jonathan Bradshaw, who has attempted various calculations to determine minimum income standards for households in the UK.[5] The last column, which (arbitrarily and crudely) counts 1 person for the first and 0.5 persons for everyone after that, frankly does as well as a guide to minimum incomes as far more sophisticated schemes – and rather better than the OECD scale used for international comparisons.

Table 4.2: Equivalence scales

	OECD scale	Minimum Income Standard	Minimum Income Standard with childcare	Flat scale of 0.5 after first person
Single	1.00	1.00	1.00	1.00
Couple	1.49	1.46	1.46	1.50
Single pensioner	1.00	0.89	0.89	1.00
Couple pensioner	1.49	1.26	1.26	1.50
Couple + 1 (aged 1)	1.79	1.68	2.36	2.00
Couple + 2 (aged 3/8)	2.09	2.13	3.08	2.50
Couple + 3 (aged 3/8/14)	2.58	2.65	3.58	3.00
Couple + 4 (aged 1/3/8/14)	2.88	2.82	4.11	3.50
Lone parent + 1 (aged 1)	1.30	1.31	2.00	1.50
Lone parent + 2 (aged 3/8)	1.60	1.71	2.66	2.00
Lone parent + 3 (aged 3/8/14)	2.09	2.23	3.18	2.50

Benefits are always part of a broader package; they are meaningless in isolation. It is vitally important whether there are alternative provisions for housing, childcare, medical care and so on, and the existence of other types of income can have a crucial impact. For benefits to be

[5]   J. Bradshaw (2008) 'A new equivalence scale', available at: www. minimumincomestandard.org/downloads/launch/equivalence_ WP3_20june08.pdf

adequate, they do not all necessarily have to be set at the same specified level. It is only possible to arrive at a final target income if the system is designed to produce that income, and that implies a particular kind of benefit system, based on income testing and income thresholds. That is not a good model, for all the reasons outlined in Chapter Three. The level of benefit to be paid needs to be appropriate in its own terms. If, when it is added together with other parts of the income package, it leads to differences in total incomes, then that has to be accepted.

Changing benefit incomes

It is not easy to work out, from information about benefit rates alone, what a person's total income is likely to be. The first problem, obviously enough, is that people can have income from different sources – present employment, past employment, relatives, non-dependants, investment income, occasional work and so on. Incomes fluctuate, and means testing is unavoidably complicated and difficult to administer: the ideal of a 'guaranteed minimum' is not difficult to achieve if benefits offer at least that minimum, but if governments want to offer no more than the minimum, the situation becomes unmanageable. There is a long history of benefits of this sort. They are complicated, confusing, people do not receive them who should and people do receive them who should not.

The second problem is that entitlement to one benefit can affect entitlement to another. Several benefits are treated as 'earnings replacement' benefits: they are not necessarily means-tested, but because earnings only get replaced once, only one of them can be paid at a time. They include the State Pension, contributory Jobseekers Allowance (JSA) and Employment and Support Allowance (ESA), bereavement benefits and Carer's Allowance. Sometimes, benefits act as a 'passport' to others, such as free school meals. Some local authorities still wrongly suspend payments of Housing Benefit when people lose entitlement to qualifying benefits,[6] but Housing Benefit

---

[6]   See, for example, Upper Tribunal, Cases CH/3736/2006 and CH/1664/2009.

was always supposed to be available in and out of work, and loss of the qualifying benefit is not a good reason to suspend payments. In administrative terms, the main problems arise during transitions – changes in circumstances. In principle, it should not be difficult to establish that people get either ESA or JSA when they are workless, but ESA claimants who are judged fit to work are not simply transferred to JSA – they are told to register a further claim, adding a layer of complexity to the transition.

The situation is made much more complex by the range of ancillary benefits that might still be available. The most important of these is probably Housing Benefit, partly because it provides nominally large amounts (even if the claimant does not get anything from the money) but also because it has such a major impact on the 'marginal rate of deduction'. If a person's income increases, Housing Benefit alone will make sure that 65p of every extra pound of net income is clawed back. Council Tax Support (in Scotland, Council Tax Reduction) generally pulls back another 20%, not counting tax or National Insurance contributions. The new Universal Credit system will be slightly more moderate than the combined withdrawal of Housing Benefit and Tax Credits, but it still withdraws 65%.

This sort of problem cannot be resolved if the objective is to make sure that people finish up with a specific total income, because the total can only be arrived at through comprehensive knowledge of a person's circumstances. Ignoring the total income, and looking only at how much money might be made available in benefits, makes the situation much more manageable; that only calls on benefits agencies to know what they are paying out. It is possible to have benefits claimed and paid entirely independently of each other, disregarding other benefit income. This is what happens now with Child Benefit: instead of making an allowance for children and knocking the value of Child Benefit off it, the benefit is simply ignored for other calculations, and the whole system is better and clearer for doing it that way.

Providing a basic income

The language of 'basic income' is widely used to refer to a specific set of proposals for a universal, unconditional Citizens' Income. Some of those issues are considered later in Chapter Six. In the first instance, however, it makes more sense to refer to 'basic' income in its literal sense: an income that offers a foundation that can be supplemented in different ways. Because benefits can be put together in different ways, the first task is to ensure that people get some element in their income package that provides basic social security – a source of income that is reliable, predictable and secure. Attempts to use means testing to provide a stable basic income have largely been self-defeating – the element of instability is built into the principle of means testing. It is worth noting, even so, that in the past there have been means-tested benefits that were designed to minimise fluctuations – six-month entitlement periods for Family Income Supplement (long gone) and older versions of Housing Benefit, as well as a five-year assessment for Pension Credit (a concession that is now in the process of being terminated).

A much better model is provided by the State Pension. The State Pension is admittedly complex – probably more complex than it needs to be. A confusing calculation based on past contributions – rarely disputed, because it depends on lifetime career records – has been replaced for new pensions with a simpler test based on the number of contributory years. However, there are several benefits bundled into the pension, including the State Pension itself, some allowances for dependants (also being phased out: they apply to people who claimed before April 2016), transitional entitlements related to the former State Second Pension and a universal element for those above the age of 80. This is hardly a model of clarity, and there is no reason to suppose that it all makes sense to claimants – but it works. It provides a core, regular income for millions of people, delivered with rapid, effective administration and a minimum of fuss. It has also, remarkably, managed to provide pensions uncontroversially – the general criticisms that are applied to other benefits, such as cost, dependency, lifestyle choices and fraud, are hardly mentioned.

Contributory benefits have played a central role in ensuring adequate incomes for pensioners. The core problem with depending on contributions more broadly is that they leave gaps. Unemployment benefits failed partly because of mass unemployment, but more generally because at the lower end of the job market, people did not get contributions paid. Short-term sickness benefits might have worked, but they had the same weakness as unemployment benefits, and the primary responsibility was transferred to statutory sick pay over thirty years ago. Longer-term sickness benefits, now carried forward in ESA, lump together a range of conditions that are difficult to cover by insurance: people who are chronically sick and disabled from birth; people who need to retire early; people whose sick pay does not cover their circumstances; and people who are unemployed while suffering from a range of conditions.

There is a stronger case for using universal provision to offer a foundational income. Child Benefit is the most important example. It goes to all families with children aged up to 16, and to those at school up to 19; as the school leaving age increases, it will go increasingly to children in that age group. Like the State Pension, Child Benefit offers a long-term, stable income with a relative minimum of fuss. It is not immune from problems. In the past, the main problems – largely resolved – have been:

- the deduction of Child Benefit from other benefits – that largely ended in 2004;
- confusion about which partner in a divorce was entitled to claim (there used, for example, to be a highly confusing law based on days that left couples with shared responsibility with reduced entitlement); and
- the application of a cohabitation rule to the premiums for single parents.

Recent reforms have introduced new complications, notably:

- the application of a differential rule for families with higher earners, which adds layers of complexity and threatens the continued entitlement of families with fluctuating earnings; and
- the inclusion of Child Benefit in the 'benefit cap', which, though it affects very few people, mainly complicates calculations for families with children claiming high Housing Benefit.

Child Benefit is often claimed to have almost full take-up. That is difficult to verify – there are rules against backdating, and some people do seem to delay, in particular, for their first claim. The successes of the system rest in its simplicity, its coverage, its distributive impact – it has a major effect both on income poverty for families with children and for the stability of incomes – and the fact that it does not interact with other benefits.

Unfortunately, universality does not have the degree of political acceptance that extends to pensions. There are routine condemnations of the system in the press[7] and the principle of paying the benefit universally to better-off families has been described as 'bonkers'.[8] *The Times* has described Winter Fuel Payment as 'indefensible' and 'daft'.[9]

The distributive effects of universal benefits are easy to defend. Atkinson shows that, mathematically speaking, it is generally possible to get the same results from altering the tax threshold and the tax rate, by tapering benefits, or by offering a basic income benefit and taxing all income.[10] The real argument here, then, is about how things are done. What is the point of churning money – taxing people with one hand and giving them benefits with the other?

[7] See: https://www.theguardian.com/society/economics-blog/2013/jan/07/child-benefit-change-economic

[8] See: http://www.dailymail.co.uk/news/article-1317438/George-Osborne-axes-child-benefit-higher-rate-taxpayers-slaps-cap-welfare.html

[9] *The Times* (2010) Winter Fool Payment, 14th October, p 2.

[10] A.B. Atkinson (1983) *The economics of inequality*, Oxford: Oxford University Press.

There are moral arguments, some of them rather grandiose, but the best reasons are practical ones. Where there is an income tax and a universal benefit, people need to be asked about their income once. Where there is income tax and a means-tested benefit, people still need to be asked once, but others will have to be asked twice. Older people commonly have to fill in forms about tax, Pension Credit, Council Tax Benefit and Housing Benefit – and some politicians think that is not enough. Millions of adults of working age have to fill in forms about tax and tax credits, and then another 5 million have to fill in forms about JSA and ESA. When a change to Child Benefit was introduced for higher earners, it called for more than a million extra forms to be filled. This is about the distribution of the burden of administration, and who bears that burden. Taxing with one hand and allocating funds with the other is simpler, fairer, less liable to error, much less cumbersome and much less intrusive.

Universal payments like Child Benefit and Winter Fuel Payment are circumscribed and relatively predictable. By contrast with the assumption of many critics that universal benefits are massively expensive, they can be specified as tightly as a government pleases, with no risk of overspend, and much lower administrative costs than means- or needs-tested benefits. That is why some of the poorest countries on earth have been introducing Basic Health Care Packages, denying many people all manner of expensive treatments – there is no provision for older people, people with long-term disabilities or expensive high-tech medicine – but making sure that cheap, practical measures are used to save as many lives as possible.[11] Universality is often seen as a costly alternative; the opposite may be true.

[11] World Bank (1993) *World Development Report 1993: Investing in health*, Washington, DC: World Bank.

FIVE

Reforming key benefits

This book is concerned with problems and proposals for reform, and too close a focus on the mechanics of specific benefits is liable to confine the discussion and close down options. An examination of the differences between, for example, Cold Weather Payments and Winter Fuel Payment – despite their names, they are different in their structure and intention – would call for a description of each benefit, a consideration of their purposes and the issues they address, and the arguments for and against their different constructions. (Cold Weather Payments, by the way, are supplementary payments made when weather is cold; Winter Fuel Payment is a payment made to help people budget during periods when life might be more expensive, and does not depend on whether the weather is cold at all.) Once even that much has been explained, it becomes very difficult to escape from that framework, and the argument starts to be about which benefits should be retained or how they should be modified. This chapter discusses the shape of the benefits system only in much more general terms, reviewing how they work together in five main circumstances: benefits for older people, people with disabilities, family benefits, people out of work and benefits for housing.

Benefits for older people

There was a time, in the 1960s, when older people were the most deprived and disadvantaged group receiving benefits. Even in the 1970s, they constituted the largest numbers in official statistics about poverty. That has changed, partly because the composition of households in Britain has changed – young people are much more likely to form households in their own right – but also because of progressive improvements in the financial position of pensioners. Those improvements have happened because of earnings-related pensions, measures to improve the position of women and increases over time in the basic value of pensions. The extent of provision for older people, and the size of the State Pension in particular, tends to invite an assumption that older people are substantially provided for by state benefits – that there is a two-tier system, offering National Insurance pensions for most and supplementary means-tested benefits for the rest. That was largely true after the Beveridge reforms, and remained so for the best part of fifty years. The current position is better explained, however, in terms of the three tiers outlined in Chapter Four. The dividing lines between the tiers are not particularly sharp, but with the growth of occupational and private pensions, more than 80% of pensioners receive additional income beyond the level of the State Pension. The most important part of that comes from occupational pensions, held by 62% of pensioners; they are worth about three times more than private pensions, held by 19%.[1] Since the entitlements to an occupational pension depend on a fairly full work record, the same people are also likely to get the State Pension, and under the old pension rules, which still apply to most people, that would be true even if they were contracted out of the additional earnings-related element. The median value of occupational pensions is £142 per week, and when that is combined with the State Pension,

---

[1]   Pensions Policy Institute (no date) 'Pension facts', Tables 14 and 15, available at: http://www.pensionspolicyinstitute.org.uk/pension-facts/pension-facts-tables/

it more or less doubles the value; 31%, half of 62%, get more than that median figure. It makes sense, then, to think of the top third as holding a combination of good occupational pensions with a basic State Pension.

The people in the middle tier, again about a third, hold the State Pension, usually with some supplements from occupational pensions, private pensions and the state earnings-related pensions. Those additions are usually enough to mean that they will not need to claim further benefits, but the State Pension remains the largest component of the income package.

The lowest tier has only incomplete pension entitlements and has to claim low-income supplements such as Pension Credit. 4.4 million pensioners get Pension Credit, 1.4 million get Housing Benefit. (I have written about 'thirds', but the approximation is a little rough because so many of those eligible for Pension Credit do not get it. It is probably closer to think of the distribution of the three tiers as 30–30–40.)

Richard Titmuss wrote more than 60 years ago of the possible emergence of 'two nations in old age': he recognised, presciently, that 'private pensions in the future may outweigh in importance national insurance pensions'.[2] In the upper tiers, the most visible problems currently afflicting pension provision have to do with private and occupational pensions, where public policy has taken a series of wrong turns. The first has been the reliance on individual firms to provide pension funds. It should have been clear from the experience of France, where declining industries such as railways and mines had struggled to meet commitments to pensions, that even the largest firms could not guarantee to deliver pensions into the distant future. The UK system was heavily dependent on much smaller units, and they have unsurprisingly not been well enough funded. The second key problem has been about the balance of funding and 'dynamisation', or pay-as-you-go. All effective pensions schemes have been dynamised

[2]   R. Titmuss (1955) 'Pensions systems and population change', in *Essays on 'The welfare state'*, London: Allen and Unwin, 1963, p 72.

– workers now pay for pensioners now. Funded systems cannot keep pace, which is why private pensions tend to offer about a third of the benefits that occupational pensions do. The third key problem has been about the reliance on commercial providers, who want to draw profits. Richard Murphy comments that the amount of subsidy given to pension providers potentially exceeds the amount they pay out in pensions:

> something close to, and in many cases more than, the amount of tax relief given on pension fund contributions is taken by the pensions industry for the benefit of the City and the financial services industry without a penny of benefit going to potential pensioners.[3]

In the lower tier, the problems that are most prominent are probably the problems of Pension Credit; however, the need to rely on Pension Credit reflects, in its turn, a deficiency in the State Pension. The main intrinsic problem is that the basic pension relies on contributions based on people's work record: credits are given in some cases, but the condition must mean that some people do not qualify. There have been persistent problems of coverage, most obviously affecting women; these have left about one pensioner in six with the need for income supplements. Pension Credit, the means-tested alternative, is there to fill in the gaps. It works much less well, despite the long periods between assessments (now being phased out); it is particularly prone to mistakes in calculation and delivery.

The obvious way to deal with that particular problem would be to extend the coverage and increase the level of the State Pension, but it is difficult to do that and to maintain the principle that it is paid in respect of contributions. One option is to enhance and strengthen the entitlements secured by contributions, building up stronger

[3] R. Murphy (2014) 'If you want to halve the deficit abolish pension tax relief', available at: http://www.taxresearch.org.uk/Blog/2014/03/11/if-you-want-to-halve-the-deficit-abolish-pension-tax-releif/

entitlements; but this implies that people who have not been able to contribute will need residual coverage. The other is the route followed in New Zealand, where 'Superannuation' effectively gives people a citizen's pension, on minimal conditions. The Coalition government briefly considered introducing a Citizen's Pension – a basic rate for all pensioners – but ultimately opted instead for a modified contributory pension, based on the number of years that a person has contributed, which will only apply to people who newly retire and not to existing pensioners. That kind of arrangement implies that it will take forty or fifty years before the traces of the older systems finally disappear. This is not how things have to be. Despite appearances, pensions now are not generally paid for out of savings or a fund; they are paid for by contributions now. Delaying the introduction of the flat-rate pension denies support to current pensioners. A delayed introduction means that workers now are promising themselves better pensions at the expense of future generations, but that they are not ready to pay for current pensions.

It could be done differently. Rather than offering new pensions only to new pensioners, they could be offered to those who are oldest. Flat-rate pensions could be offered at first to the oldest pensioners – in the first instance, those over the age of 85 or 90. The age limit could then be lowered in incremental stages, down (say) to 80, 75, 72 or 70. That would leave an opening for independent pensions designed to supplement income specifically for younger pensioners, and for more generous universal provision for the groups of older people who have typically been most in need. The advantages of approaching the policy this way would be:

- It would direct resources in the first instance to a cohort of pensioners who are least protected by earnings-related alternatives.
- It would be fairer; it would mean that workers were not promising themselves pensions and refusing to deliver them to current pensioners.
- It would not immediately extinguish the earned entitlements of people within the Second State Pension.

- It would create an opening for alternative types of private scheme or options for saving, for example, schemes that might cover people for a fixed period, from ages 65–80 and later from 65–75.
- It would ease the thorny problem of how to increase the retirement age. Introducing the pension only for younger, new pensioners would create a situation where governments are committed to a progressively expanding scheme as younger pensioners retire, and where it might be necessary to withdraw entitlements that have previously been offered. Starting at the other end of the age distribution would mean that governments would have the choice of whether or not to lower the pension age for the State Pension further, taking into account the economic conditions of the time.

Benefits for disability

Disability benefits are there for many reasons. They include, among others:

- raising low income – people with long-term disabilities have much lower incomes than others;
- social protection/insurance;
- support for carers;
- special needs, such as mobility;
- extra costs;
- support while out of work;
- compensation for injury;
- compensation for long-term low income;
- support for rehabilitation;
- promoting employment;
- desert; and
- paying for social care.

Any reform that is based on a small handful of principles, such as extra costs and care needs, is likely to override others that are equally valid.

The current system is poorly understood. Many people who might be able to claim do not identify themselves as disabled.[4] Many of the disability benefits are mislabelled. Attendance Allowance is not given for attendance – it is a benefit for severe disability. Severe Disablement Allowance, now being phased out, is a non-contributory invalidity pension. Personal Independence Payment (PIP) is not given for independence. The care component of Disability Living Allowance (DLA) is not given to make care possible – people get it when there is no carer. Research for the Department for Work and Pensions (DWP) found that claimants of DLA often did not understand what the benefit was for.[5]

There are also anomalies in the design and delivery of existing benefits. Carer's Allowance – which, unlike Attendance Allowance, is actually given for attendance – does not go to most carers: they are excluded if they receive another 'income replacement' benefit such as a pension. This means that carers who seem to qualify might be given a note to say that they have an 'underlying entitlement' but are not actually going to get any money from it. Another rule that makes little sense in practice makes someone's age at the point where they become disabled critical in determining whether or not mobility support is available. Claimants of the mobility component of Disability Living Allowance generally receive extensions of mobility support after the age limits are reached. A third of DLA claims are made on this basis by older people, and this situation is likely to continue through the reform of DLA into PIP. The million pensioners who get DLA can get support for their mobility needs, but the 1.6 million who get Attendance Allowance cannot. It is probably true to say, too, that disability benefits also need to be considered in relation to a wider set

---

[4] DWP (no date) 'Ad hoc analysis', Tables 10–11, available at: https://www.gov.uk/government/uploads/system/uploads/attachment_data/file/210030/q1-2013-data.xls

[5] A. Thomas (2008) *Disability Living Allowance: Disallowed claims*, London: DWP, p 20.

of resources for support – health care, housing and domiciliary support – which are not necessarily best distributed through cash benefits.

Disability benefits have always been problematic. They are intrinsically selective – there has to be some test of need, because that is how we can tell that people qualify – and selectivity always leads to complications and mistakes. There have been arguments for some kind of general or 'universal' disability benefits. In the UK, the proposals initially came from the Disability Alliance; the idea was examined in more detail in Ireland by the Commission on the Status of People with Disabilities.[6] They argued for a unified benefit combining a disability pension, a payment for the extra costs of disability and allowances for carers. People found it impossible to agree on the details, and the idea was abandoned.

While there may be little hope of avoiding selectivity, it is not necessary for assessments for disability benefits to be quite as burdensome and intrusive as they are at present. As things stand, nearly everyone who claims is being assessed. According to the National Audit Office, the DWP had initially intended 75% of all claimants to undergo face-to-face assessments for PIP, but the actual rate has been 98%.[7] Although repeated checks on people with long-term conditions have now been acknowledged to be 'pointless',[8] most of the assessments that remain are little better. They either confirm the obvious or they duplicate information that is already held. Some assessments are necessary: many people with disabilities cannot say whether they are disabled or not, and have no idea whether or not their disability fits the

---

[6] Government of Ireland (1996) *Report of the Commission on the Status of People with Disabilities*, Dublin: Stationery Office.

[7] See: https://www.nao.org.uk/wp-content/uploads/2016/01/Contracted-out-health-and-disability-assessments.pdf

[8] J. Grierson (2016) 'DWP scraps restesting for chronically ill sickness benefits claimants', *Guardian*, 1 October, available at: https://www.theguardian.com/society/2016/oct/01/dwp-scraps-retesting-for-chronically-ill-sickness-benefits-claimants

criteria for benefits.[9] Any general rule, no matter how sensitively it is administered, is going to have to deal with some grey areas. However, the same approach does not have to apply to everyone.

First, it is possible to identify certain conditions that should imply automatic entitlement, offering benefits on minimal or secondary evidence – either accepting on sight that the person has a qualifying disability (double amputation, severe disfigurement) or passporting benefits on the basis of provision by other agencies (congenital disability, blindness).

Second, there are conditions that will have led to prolonged long-term contact with health services, and certification from a consultant is sufficient to establish that the condition is there without requiring further detailed examination of personal circumstances. Examples are terminal illness, multiple sclerosis, motor neurone disease, malignant neoplasms or brittle bones.

Third, there are conditions where existing services in long-term contact with the individual are far better placed to judge the impact of a condition than an independent assessor could be, and it would be appropriate to accept medical certification. Examples are continued psychosis, epilepsy, dementia and learning disability.

Only after these three categories are considered is it appropriate to think in terms of further individual assessment. The points scheme currently used in a range of benefits was initially developed from work to establish the range and severity of disabilities in the UK.[10] That research validated the approach through a range of tests, but it pointed to an important conclusion: that once the primary disabilities had been identified, it was very rare for further disabilities to make any notable difference to the findings, and that information served no useful purpose. It follows that it is neither appropriate nor necessary

---

[9] DWP (no date) 'Ad hoc analysis', Tables 10–11, available at: https://www. gov.uk/government/uploads/system/uploads/attachment_data/file/210030/ q1-2013-data.xls

[10] J. Martin, H. Meltzer and D. Elliot (1988) *The prevalence of disability among adults in Britain*, London: HMSO.

to ask most claimants whether they can go to the toilet unaided. The question is embarrassing and the information obtained is, for the most part, irrelevant. The assessment process should begin by asking people to identify their most important disabilities, ask questions about those and go further only in marginal or complex circumstances.

Finally, there will be a residual category of people who are not adequately dealt with by any of the four stages just outlined, and who will require or ask for a more thorough comprehensive assessment. This category should be small.

Family benefits

It is more difficult to discuss family benefits than most other categories, because this is not the way that policies have been constructed in the UK. 'Families' are generally taken to mean families with younger children: one of the peculiarities of the system is that adult children are treated as if they were independent households, and family carers have no distinct status. Three main benefits relate to children: Child Benefit, which is (almost) a universal benefit going to all families with dependent children; Tax Credits (nominally two benefits, which Universal Credit will eventually combine into one) for families on low incomes, including allowances for childcare costs; and Sure Start Maternity Grant for families on low income. Possibly the list should include free school meals, milk and vitamins for expectant mothers, fostering allowances from social work, and the insurance-based Guardian's Allowance.

At the same time, some family benefits have been removed: the insurance-based Maternity Allowance, which is now the responsibility of employers (other expectant mothers may have to claim ESA); One Parent Benefit, formerly an addition to Child Benefit; and Income Support, the generic benefit for people on low incomes, where mothers with young children were not required to work. There are also some visible penalties associated with family formation. Couples get less than two independent adults who share a household, so there is a cohabitation rule. Universal Credit offers financial support for couples but demands commitments from both adults individually.

From April 2017, the allowances for several benefits will take into account no more than two children, as a penalty to people who have more; because families pool resources, that is effectively a reduction for all the children. The message that seems to come over from politicians and the media is that family formation is an individual choice, and that there is something deeply irresponsible about having more children than one can pay for. There is a recurrent myth that people opt to live a life on benefits and have children as a way of increasing their benefits. It is difficult to disprove this from larger numbers, but it is possible to say that it runs counter to general experience. Larger families tend to be older families (because it takes time to have a larger family). They come to benefits for other reasons – typically unemployment, disability or divorce – after a change in circumstances. Much the biggest group of people who get long-term benefits are older people with disabilities, and they are less likely to have young children than others. Overall, while some families do have children while in receipt of benefits, families who get benefits for longer periods are markedly less likely than others to have more children.

There is equally an assumption that people who have lots of children gets lots of benefits, and that those benefits will be lost if people work. For the most part, this is not so; it is not how most benefits are constructed. Most of the allowances for dependent children on income-tested benefits have disappeared. People get Child Benefit whether they work or not. The main effect of having a larger family is either to change the calculation of Housing Benefit and Tax Credits, or to change the size of house that a family needs. Their rules apply to people in or out of work. As it turns out, there are not many 'large' families on benefits. The information is not regularly available, but Channel 4 researchers found the figures from a Freedom of Information request.[11] In May 2011, there were:

---

[11]   See: http://blogs.channel4.com/factcheck/factcheck-the-truth-about-the-child-benefits-cap/11739

   1,354,280 families with children in receipt of benefits;
     194,220 with three children;
      76,310 with four;
      25,980 with five;
       8,780 with six;
       3,200 with seven;
       1,080 with eight;
         360 with nine;
         130 with ten; and
          50 with eleven or more.

Large families were far more common in the decades before the welfare state. The tiny numbers of very large families still seem to be enough to fuel the venom of the press.[12]

In the absence of any visible 'family policy', it is hard to know what to advocate for family benefits. Discussions tend to get diverted into more general issues, such as low income and work status. Possibly the easiest way to imagine a different way of doing things might be to look at the benefits available in another country. For much of the post-war period – at least until the late 1980s – French social policy treated family support as the central purpose of benefits, while poverty was hardly considered. The system in France offers a range of benefits, including:

- *Allocations familiales*, a benefit for each child;
- *Prestation d'acceuil de jeune enfant*, a supplement for newborn children or children being adopted;
- *Majoration*, an addition for children over 14 in families of two or more children;

[12] See: http://www.dailymail.co.uk/news/article-2083998/Benefit-cap-190-families-10-children-cost-taxpayers-11m-A-YEAR.html; http://www.dailymail.co.uk/news/article-2306741/Jobless-mother-10-vows-having-babies-despite-cuts-30-000-year-benefits.html; and http://www.dailymail.co.uk/news/article-3087519/So-m-effing-dole-Mother-ten-children-five-fathers-wants-50-grandchildren-benefits-rolling-in.html

- *Allocation forfaitaire provisoire*, where an older child remains resident in the family household;
- *Allocation soutien familial*, for children lacking one or both parents;
- *Aide à la garde d'enfants pour parents isolés*, to help lone parents with childcare costs; and
- *Carte familles nombreuses*, giving travel concessions for large families.

As a general proposition, the various benefits all have the same payday, so that different families receive their different amounts at predictable points of time.

The example of France points to several ways that benefits might be designed differently. It would make sense to have benefits available for a range of family circumstances, for example:

- a benefit for families with children under the age where childcare is generally available, currently four years;
- a benefit for children with disabilities; and
- a benefit for children who lack the support of one or both parents.

Any of these, however, could stumble on a difference of moral perception: the question of who is responsible for the welfare of children. Many current policies are residual and focus on individual, 'troubled' families: problems in families, low income, non-employment and poor educational attainment are overwhelmingly attributed to the individuals who suffer from them. The case has to be made to reconsider how family benefits could relate to the social structure.

Out of work

Over the last few years, policy for 'welfare reform' has focused on one central idea: that benefits have to be designed to get people into work. The starting point for that assumption lies in the misconception that benefits are mainly there to provide for people out of work. That is plainly wrong: benefits are there for lots of reasons, and work is a small part of them. Most benefits go to older people – not just pensions, but a big slice of benefits for housing and disability. So, everything that follows in a section about work is subject to a basic qualification: it has to be about the lesser part of the system, which goes to people of working age. Next, more than half of those benefits go to people who are in work on the same terms as they go to people out of work. Tax credits, Housing Benefit, Child Benefit and most benefits for disability go to people regardless of their work status. This does mean that some proportion will go to people who are not working, but they will also be paid to people who are working – and half the low-income families in the UK have someone who is working.

As Income Support is being phased out, the only benefits that are focused on people who are not working are Jobseekers Allowance (JSA), ESA and Carer's Allowance. Carer's Allowance can be dealt with fairly rapidly in this context – this is for people who are excluded from the obligation to look for work because they have to spend time instead looking after a disabled person. There have been other benefits that make this sort of exemption, and maybe there will be again: Income Support was used to support mothers of young children to stay at home to look after them, and Educational Maintenance Allowance was designed to encourage children to stay at school rather than putting themselves on the job market. The main focus on supporting people into work falls, however, on the first two benefits – JSA and ESA. Although those two benefits have similarities in their design, and they are in the process of being combined into Universal Credit, they have a very different role and purpose.

Jobseekers Allowance JSA is an income replacement benefit for people who are unemployed. It has two main components: an insurance-based benefit for the first six months of employment, and a means-tested benefit that covers both short- and long-term needs. The old system of Unemployment Benefit, which JSA replaced in 1995, had mechanisms to pay people for days of casual unemployment and short-time working; JSA does not, which is particularly important in view of the growth of casualised, 'zero-hours' contracts. It is probably true to say that JSA is increasingly seen as a form of support for long-term unemployment – which makes little sense, because the substantial majority of JSA claimants find work within a year. Unemployment benefits mainly cover people who are unemployed for the short term, and they need to cover people for the interruption of earnings. It would make sense at least to have a higher rate for the first year of unemployment, and a different benefit for people unemployed in the longer term.

It has always been a condition of unemployment benefits that people are expected to work when the opportunity arises, and that failure to take advantage of a job opportunity is grounds for denying benefit. For most of the last seventy years, this could have led to a penalty of up to six weeks, later replaced by a penalty of up to 26 weeks. The Coalition government replaced those sanctions with a much stricter set, including fixed period penalties of great length. People may have benefit stopped for a month or three months for being five minutes late for an appointment; repeated problems lead to penalties of six months or three years. The steep increase in sanctions after May 2010 continued until late 2013, when it started to decline.[13] At the highest point, more than a fifth of all unemployed claimants in Britain had had their benefit stopped for an extended period of time during the previous year.

Employment and Support Allowance The largest benefit for people 'out of work' is not for people who are unemployed, but for people who are too ill to work. ESA has become a major focus of political criticisms. Its numbers went up in the 1990s and they have remained determinedly high ever since. The picture is not quite what the official statistics seem to show: the Labour government changed the way that ESA is counted retrospectively in order to bring together figures for everyone on long-term invalidity support. The figures include people

[13] D. Webster (2016) 'Explaining the rise and fall of JSA and ESA sanctions 2010–16', available at: http://www.cpag.org.uk/sites/default/files/uploads/16-08%20Supplement%20-%20Reasons%20for%20rise%20%20fall%203%20Oct%2016.docx

receiving Incapacity Benefit, Income Support and Severe Disablement Allowance. That makes it look as if the figures jumped by a million under Labour, but, in fact, they remained fairly constant.

Several groups are lumped together in ESA claims: some have sicknesses that they can reasonably hope to be temporary; some have disadvantages that they might reasonably hope to overcome. A substantial number of claimants are older males who are unable to do manual labour. ESA undoubtedly contains a high level of hidden unemployment – unwell people with limited capacity who would prefer to work if such opportunities existed – and others say that they would like to work in the future.[14] That does not necessarily mean that they are ready to work immediately. On the contrary, the central purpose of the benefit is to provide for people who it is not reasonable to expect to work – that is how the benefit is defined in the statute.

The standard that is applied to assess this is the Work Capability Assessment (WCA). This is a very restrictive test, which has proved highly problematic; it seeks to determine residual capability for work rather than the extent of someone's illness, and medical evidence about illness is consequently liable to be dismissed. Hundreds of thousands of people have been declared fit for work, most have appealed (many successfully, if only their cases get to be heard); several thousand have died, in some cases, very shortly after being declared fit. The people who pass the WCA are classified into two groups: the 'support group', who have no work requirements; and a 'work-related activity group' (WRAG), who are expected to prepare themselves for re-entry to the labour market. There may be people for whom this is appropriate – for example, some people recovering from mental illness – but the category has been used as a catch-all, not as a way of ensuring that people are supported appropriately. The government has never defined who ought to be in the WRAG; the way the rules work is that people are admitted to the support group and the rest are assumed to require work-related activity. That directly contradicts, of course, the terms

---

[14] P. Alcock, C. Beatty, S. Fothergill, R. Macmillan and S. Yeandle (2003) *Work to welfare*, Cambridge: Cambridge University Press.

of the assessment, which has already established that the person is not capable of work. If someone has a stroke and is relearning to walk, there is every reason to excuse that person from the ability to work now. There may well be reason to hope that in the course of a few months, it may be possible for that person to recover sufficiently to start work again, but that does not mean that they can get out of bed today. The whole point of ESA is that it is meant to be there for people who it is not reasonable to expect to work. If it is not reasonable for them to work, it is not reasonable for them to be made to do things that look, feel, sound or taste like work either.

ESA deals with a range of circumstances, which the primary distinction between support and work-related activity fails to reflect. Part of ESA is a sickness benefit. Most people who are sick while employed will get statutory sick pay; some will not, and they get ESA instead. The same is true for women who fall ill while pregnant. The bulk of ESA claimants, however, are people who are long-term sick – whose illnesses last for more than six months – and have no employment. That figure will include some people who have a disability and who are unemployed; it is in their interests to claim ESA rather than JSA because the benefit is higher and the conditions are less stringent. There are also some people who are very severely disabled; they used to get Severe Disablement Allowance but their numbers have been bundled in with the ESA figures. The final main group of people to mention are people who are effectively in retirement, in advance of pension age. If a teacher or a civil servant becomes sick later in their career, they will often be able to draw on an occupational pension. For people who do not have that option – a substantial number of claimants are older males who are unable to do manual labour – ESA is the main opportunity they have to get an income. The different circumstances probably ought to be operated under different rules, and so different benefits:

- sickness where statutory sick pay is not available;
- incapacity and reduced capacity for work;
- long-term disability; and
- early retirement on the grounds of ill-health.

Universal Credit Universal Credit is not, in theory, an out-of-work benefit. It was intended to bring together six benefits – JSA, ESA, Working Tax Credit, Child Tax Credit, Housing Benefit and Income Support. Dovetailing benefits in and out of work was supposed to make it easier for people to move into work (a situation that is scarcely appropriate for recipients of ESA). Much of the original idea has been eroded: the staggering incompetence in the development of the programme has led to a 'reset' of the whole programme and successive delays. While the programme was originally intended to be operational by 2017, and should have been received by at least 7 million people, by August 2016, there were just under 325,000 claimants.[15]

Most of the failures of Universal Credit are attributable to an inadequate concept, compounded by weaknesses in the design.[16] Among the many failures of Universal Credit are the following:

- All the primary objectives – such as simplification, work incentives, reducing in-work poverty, smoothing transitions and cutting back on fraud and error – have been fatally compromised.
- There is no effective system for coordinating and pooling all the information required in one place – the new system has come to rely primarily on returns from claimants about changes.
- The marginal rate of deduction is much higher than intended.
- The system makes complex demands of people (for example, those relating to security, agreements by couples and job search), which are almost impossible to police.
- The 'work allowances' have been cut back, especially for single people, so that there will be no financial interest in maintaining contact with the benefit system once a recipient has started work.

[15] DWP (2016) 'Universal Credit Statistics', available at: https://www.gov.uk/government/statistics/universal-credit-29-apr-2013-to-1-sept-2016

[16] See P. Spicker (2013) 'Introducing Universal Credit', in G. Ramia, K. Farnsworth and Z. Irving (eds) *Social Policy Review 25*, Bristol: The Policy Press, pp 3–22.

Activation The idea of 'activation' comes from Denmark, where the 1997 Act on Active Social Policy claimed that it would 'activate' claimants by getting them to accept more responsibility for work search. In Britain, the language of Labour's 'welfare reform' was couched in terms of rights and responsibilities: people had rights to benefit, but those rights were dependent on reciprocal responsibilities and duties, including the duty to actively look for work. In the UK system, those responsibilities are enshrined in the Jobseekers Agreement – and imposed on the claimant, because the terms of the commitment, including its language, are determined by the secretary of state. Those terms now include 35 hours of job search in a week, enrolment into training programmes or work-related assignments, and sometimes mandatory work activity. More than half the claimants think that some part of the commitment that they have been forced to sign is unreasonable[17] (but, of course, they have to sign it nevertheless).

A great deal of emphasis has been put on schemes to improve 'employability' and readiness for work. The schemes offer mentoring, training and work experience; the latest incarnation is the Work Programme. The early evidence on the Work Programme was that it seemed to be slowing down the rate at which people returned to work.[18] The initial effect of sending large numbers of referrals, moderated to some extent in recent months, was to flood the agencies involved in the work with large numbers of people that the programmes could do nothing with, and there were accusations that what they have ended up doing is throwing people randomly at available jobs in the hope that something would stick.[19] Current

---

[17] D. Webster (2015) Briefing on the government's response to the House of Commons Work & Pensions Committee Report on Sanctions', available at: http://www.cpag.org.uk/sites/default/files/uploads/HofC%20Sanctions%20 Govt%20Response%20DW%20Briefing%204%20Nov%202015_0.docx

[18] J. Portes (2012) 'Work experience: does it work?', available at: http:// notthetreasuryview.blogspot.com/2012/02/work-experience-does-it-work. html

[19] House of Commons Work and Pensions Committee (2013) 'Can the Work Programme work for all users?', HC 162.

figures suggest that the Work Programme has been able to place a limited number of people, but the results are disappointing for most: about a fifth of people referred have some sort of job outcome after 12 months, and after two years, two-thirds of the people on the Work Programme return to Jobcentre Plus.[20] If the aim is to improve employment prospects, the scheme has failed. However, it is not clear that that really is the objective. Far more important has been its role in disciplining claimants, and the scheme has led to far more claimants being sanctioned for non-compliance than being offered any employment opportunities.[21]

Benefit schemes are primarily concerned in practice with protecting income during spells of unemployment. Most unemployed people do not have problems of engagement, and left to their own devices, would be back at work fairly promptly. Supportive schemes potentially have an important role in engaging people who are disadvantaged, excluded and hard to reach. However, the systems of support have been undermined by their association with disciplinary measures, and unemployment protection has been undermined by the imposition of penal conditions on large numbers of unemployed people. Combining employability support with the benefits system has been detrimental to both.

Unemployment is not a single, easily explicable phenomenon: there are many reasons why people might find themselves without work, and other reasons why, if they do, they might need to claim benefits. Some unemployment is frictional, happening when people change jobs; some is casual because the kind of work that people do is not consistently available day by day. There is seasonal unemployment,

---

[20] DWP (2016) 'Quarterly Work Programme national statistics to June 2016', available at: https://www.gov.uk/government/uploads/system/uploads/attachment_data/file/554546/work-programme-statistics-to-june-2016.pdf

[21] D. Webster (2015) 'Briefing: the DWP's JSA/ESA sanctions statistics release', available at: http://www.cpag.org.uk/sites/default/files/uploads/HofC%20Sanctions%20Govt%20Response%20DW%20Briefing%204%20Nov%202015_0.docx

because some kinds of work depend on agriculture or construction, and some is cyclical, reflecting changes in the demand for labour throughout the industrial cycle. Much unemployment is invisible because the people who will take jobs that are offered – women at home, students, older people – only appear to do so when the jobs are actually available.

Despite the reservations, it is possible to make some fairly broad generalisations about unemployment. The first is this: the primary determinant of unemployment is the state of the economy. In the period since 1948, there have been three major surges in claims – the early to mid-1980s, the early 1990s and the crisis of 2008. Those surges had nothing to do with changes in benefits.

Second, there is no evidence to link the overall level of unemployment with the degree of individual effort that people invest in job search. There is some (contentious) evidence that people may move into work a little more rapidly if the benefit conditions demand it – in economic terms, that is not always a good thing, because it implies mismatches – but that does not mean that more jobs are created. The process of looking for jobs becomes a sort of game of musical chairs: the fastest, the strongest and the ones who can seize an advantage get to the chairs first, but at the end of the round, there will still be people left with nowhere to go.

Third, for the vast majority of claimants, unemployment is temporary. The poll referred to in Chapter Two found that people think about half those who claim JSA stay on it for more than a year. However, 70% of claimants return to work within the year – that figure is worse than it used to be – and relatively few people are on JSA for five years. The figures for the duration of claims were given earlier in Table 2.1: of 786,000 claimants of JSA, 39,700 have been on JSA for five years or more. Those figures look much worse than comparable figures from five years beforehand, which is partly because they reflect the economic slump since 2008, but mainly because the rolls have been swollen by people being transferred from ESA when they are too sick to work.

If the government really wanted to get people into work, there are several things that it could do that it is not doing at present. Most governments in developed countries knew what to do to get full employment after the Second World War, and most of them did it. This was done through a combination of economic management in order to ensure that demand and growth were sustained, as well as public employment. However, a myth has taken hold: that government cannot create real jobs. The World Bank's *World development report 2013* claimed, for example, that 'it is not the role of governments to create jobs … as a general rule it is the private sector that creates jobs'.[22] This is ideological codswallop. Britain needs more police, doctors, cleaners, teachers, janitors, street and park wardens, nurses, and carers. Those are real jobs, and governments can provide them.

There are good reasons to expand public employment:

- It is better for the economy for people to be working. Keynes argued that unemployment benefits were wasteful, but public works could be productive.[23] Unemployment hampers an economy. It costs money to keep people out of work; people can only pay tax if they are earning.
- Public employment reduces poverty and inequality. The higher the level of government employment, the less poverty there is. The data in Figure 5.1 were taken from Organisation for Economic Cooperation and Development (OECD) statistics for 2010/11.
- It is better for people who would otherwise be out of work. Instead of punishing people for not finding work that is not there, people could be rewarded for doing the work that is.
- There are things that need to happen: there are too few houses for the population; services for older people and mental health are woefully short of trained staff; there is not enough childcare, and

---

[22] World Bank (2013) *World development report 2013: Jobs*, Washington, DC: World Bank, p 21.

[23] J.M. Keynes (1936) *The general theory of employment, interest and money*, London: Macmillan.

that which is available is excessively expensive; Britain's public spaces are crumbling; and there is a strong case to invest in people, and investment in builders, plumbers, painters, gardeners or people to mend roads could do a power of good.

Figure 5.1: Public employment and poverty in the OECD

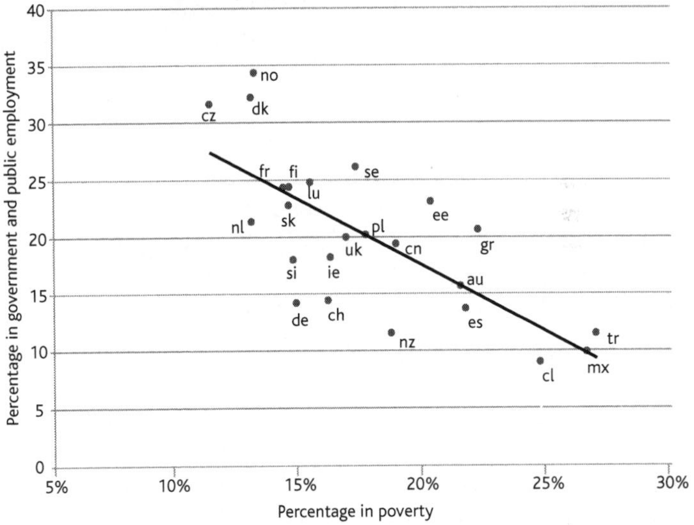

Creating more employment needs to be treated as a principle, rather than a target. The political parties like to pluck figures from the air — a million jobs, two million. Any precise figure is arbitrary. We know that 10,000 public sector jobs will be better than none, that 50,000 will be better than 10,000, that 500,000 will be better than 100,000, and so on. However, we also know that jobs need to be resourced, that people need to be trained and equipped, and that we want to be sure that money is being spent in the right places. The best answer about numbers is this: we need a lot more than we have now. The public sector needs to gradually expand until it is clear that there are enough people employed to do the work.

Benefits for housing

The last part of this general discussion is, in some ways, an anomaly. Benefits for housing are not just a matter for the benefits system; they overlap immediately and directly with housing policy. They are not the only example of using the benefits system to pay for a core service – there was a period when residential care for elderly people was paid for out of Supplementary Benefit, and childcare is being financed out of tax credits – but Housing Benefit has taken on a life of its own, becoming the third-largest benefit in the system after the State Pension and Tax Credits. The origins of Housing Benefit lie in the provision of council housing, which was financed to deliver highly subsidised rents. Some economists believed that aid given to individuals must be more efficient, and better able to promote a market, than subsidies granted to housing. The first step was taken in the 1970s with the introduction of Rent Rebate and Rent Allowance, increasing council rents, paying people large amounts in benefits to pay for the higher rents and permitting private tenants to receive an equivalent benefit. The second step, 'unified' Housing Benefit, combined those systems with the payment of rent for people on low incomes, who formerly had received rent as part of Supplementary Benefit. The third, more gradual stage has been a deliberate policy between 2002 and 2015 to increase social and council housing rents – a policy for 'rent convergence' in England based on progressive phased increases in rent.[24] The rents have still not converged, and possibly never will, but the cost of Housing Benefit has risen by about 50% since that policy started.

The fundamental issue that provision for housing costs has to address is that benefit rates were initially intended to be minimally adequate. What that meant was never clearly specified, but the initial benefit rates for major benefits bore a (tenuous) relationship to figures used in

[24] House of Commons Library (2016) 'Rent setting: social housing (England)', available at: http://researchbriefings.parliament.uk/ResearchBriefing/Summary/SN01090

the 1930s in Rowntree's studies of poverty,[25] and while it was claimed that benefits should be adequate to meet people's basic needs, it was never supposed that that should include housing costs. People who rented generally received support from National Assistance and then Supplementary Benefit; owner-occupiers received assistance with mortgages through the same systems. Housing Benefit played a major part in establishing some major principles in benefit administration. One was the gradual withdrawal of benefits as income increased. This meant that income could be relatively high before benefit ceased altogether; it also meant that people could not easily work out whether they were entitled or when their entitlement was likely to cease. The second big change was the transfer of responsibility to local authorities – many of which struggled to cope with a sudden and staggering workload. The third major change was in the finance of social housing, which had to be geared to rental returns rather than to grants. One of the greatest obstacles to the future reform of Housing Benefit is that the finance of social housing now depends on it. It is easy enough to say that Housing Benefit should be scaled down, and that funds should again be diverted into direct subsidies for low-cost housing. However, it is extraordinarily difficult to see how that could work and what could be put in its place.

---

[25]   J. Veit Wilson (1992) 'Muddle or mendacity? The Beveridge Committee and the poverty line', *Journal of Social Policy*, vol 21, no 3, pp 269–302.

SIX

Changing the benefits system

What kind of social security system should there be? When the Welfare State was introduced, there was a conscious, deliberate attempt to distance the system from the kinds of behaviour that had gone before: establishing rights, reducing administrative discretion, ending local differences and limiting the scope for personal interactions which may be demeaning. Rights are rules and norms that govern the behaviour of other people towards the person who holds them. Some rights are particular to the individual in question – occupational pension rights, for example, are typically earned through people's work records and personal to each person holding rights. Other rights are general, applying to every citizen. Much of the social security system is based on the rights of citizenship. In moral terms, that implies a general network of support based on a shared status and mutual responsibility. For practical purposes, it implies principles and rules that are operated consistently, predictably and securely for everyone. However, as the system has shifted towards more complex personal interactions, and arguably to more negative views of service users, the focus has become more blurred. Benefits agencies have taken to referring to claimants as 'customers', on the grounds that it could help to orient their work towards personal service. Customers have a relationship with providers that is voluntary and contingent; one of the main options that customers have is the option of exit. The term is not very appropriate; it fails to describe the relationship between social security provision and the citizen.

The Scottish Parliament's Welfare Reform Committee has suggested a range of principles that ought to be applied. They sum it up in the word-cloud in Figure 6.1. Some of the principles, such as treating people with dignity and respect, are difficult to disagree with. The fact that they have to be mentioned at all is worth remarking. Umberto Eco once observed that the rules that agencies introduce are generally chosen because they are the ones most likely to be broken. The list does not suggest that benefits administration needs to be comprehensive, competent or honest, because it is all of those things already. By contrast, it is often not respectful, consistent or supportive, so those are the virtues that have to be emphasised.

Figure 6.1: Scottish proposals for the principles of a reformed system

While acknowledging the force of these principles, some of the arguments in this book point in a different direction. One of the key obsessions of welfare reform has been the pursuit of 'personalisation', represented in the chart as 'person-centred' benefits. Personalised benefits are supposed to respond rapidly and flexibly to the circumstances of individuals. This is not always a good thing. Personalised benefits rely on claimants providing information about themselves that is up-to-date, accurate and clear. Life is just not like that. Many benefit claimants live with constant changes. They move in and out of work; their income goes up and down unpredictably. People who are working in casual, temporary, 'flexible' jobs do not know when or whether they will be working, when they are paid, or if they will be. People who are self-employed often do not have a clue how much they have earned or are about to earn – the Institute of Chartered Accountants warned the government that asking for returns every month was hardly likely to work when people could not make annual returns without specialist help.[1] But this goes beyond income. Many people do not know if they are in a stable personal relationship or not (not knowing might reasonably be taken to indicate that it is not stable, but that is not how the benefits authorities read it). People with disabilities cannot say whether they are disabled. Wherever there are personalised tests – whether people can bend over, read a map, use a toothbrush – the system becomes complicated and intrusive. Personalisation is presumptuous: it relies on the benefits agencies holding vast amounts of information about individuals. It is also unreliable because situations are liable to change, and it is expensive to run. Individualised, personal responses are difficult, often unfair and do not work well. 'Common sense', like the mantras of work and activation, often leads us astray.

---

[1] Institute of Chartered Accountants (2013) 'HC 576 Progress towards the implementation of Universal Credit: written evidence submitted by the Institute of Chartered Accountants for England and Wales', available at: http://www.publications.parliament.uk/pa/cm201213/cmselect/cmworpen/writev/576/m53.htm

The desire for benefits that are 'simple', 'consistent' and 'fair' runs contrary to this – but there are limits to how far the system can be simplified, or should be. Benefits do not have to be 'joined-up', as the chart suggests, because money is fungible – what matters is whether they make sense to the recipient. One of the repeated failures of social security policy in Britain has been the attempt to simplify systems by creating massive catch-all benefits – benefits that are trying to cover lots of different contingencies. Supplementary Benefit used to include elements of benefit that are now in Jobseekers Allowance (JSA), Employment and Support Allowance (ESA), Pension Credit, Income Support, Carer's Allowance, Council Tax Support, Housing Benefit and local welfare assistance. In that case, the inclusion of all these circumstances might be seen as accidental – National Assistance and then Supplementary Benefit just grew and grew – but portmanteau benefits, the sort that carry lots of different systems in one big package, have also been built deliberately. One example is Housing Benefit, which initially brought together Rent Allowance, Rent Rebate, Supplementary Benefit for rent and Rate Rebate into one baffling, fiendishly complicated cocktail. Another example is the current development of Universal Credit, which is bringing together JSA, ESA, Income Support, Housing Benefit, Working Tax Credit and Child Tax Credit – a collection that is eerily reminiscent of the functions formerly collected in Supplementary Benefit. Lumping together smaller benefits into one big benefit does not make the operation any simpler. It also means that if something goes wrong and claimants lose entitlement to benefit, the suspension of all the components together can be catastrophic.

Universal Basic Income

Many arguments have been made over the years in favour of a Universal Basic Income (UBI): a universal, unconditional payment made to every person. The case for UBI is:

- *Moral* UBI is seen as an expression of the rights of citizenship, community solidarity, social justice and a way of supporting individual dignity.
- *Economic* UBI offers people an economic springboard, choice about how to use their labour, security and predictable income in circumstances where labour markets have become increasingly precarious. UBI is often challenged on the basis that people will have no incentive to work, but there is not much evidence to support that contention. On the one hand, state pensions have reduced the proportion of people over 65 who continue to work; on the other hand, societies with more generous welfare systems also tend to have higher participation in the labour market. There is very little specific evidence; besides, it is not obvious that if some people did choose to withdraw from the labour market, it would have negative effects.
- *Practical* UBI is, in Bob Goodin's choice phrase, 'minimally presumptuous'.[2] It should be much easier to administer and deliver than existing benefits. Selective benefits are complex, inefficient and fail to reach many people that they are intended for; UBI should be simple and comprehensive.
- *Social justice* UBI is fundamentally egalitarian; if paid for by a progressive tax system, it should also be redistributive. The main criticism of this point has been that universality is potentially regressive: paying for a UBI would call for a massive extension of benefits to the better off.

The evidence for UBI has gathered strength in recent years as new systems of cash assistance have been developed across a swathe of countries in developing or transitional economies. Much of that assistance has been conditional, but while the effect of the conditions is questionable, the benefits of providing people with an income have been clear. They include better nutrition, better sanitation,

---

[2] R.E. Goodin (1992) 'Towards a minimally presumptuous social welfare policy', in P. van Parijs (ed) *Arguing for basic income*, London: Verso.

more education, better health and stronger economic engagement. These are not arguments, however, that can easily be translated into the developed economies, where there are already established systems for social security. Where there is already a minimum income, the advocates of a UBI have to show not that it is better for people to have an income, but that this is a better way to deliver it.

Various basic income schemes have been put forward for the UK. The best known scheme is probably the one put forward by the Citizens Income Trust,[3] but there have been many others. Table 6.1 outlines suggestions from four.[4] This is only a selection from a much wider range of schemes, but they share common defects. None of them would achieve the promised advantages of a UBI. There would be critical weaknesses in the way they are financed, their relationship to existing benefits and their impact on claimants.

One of the central problems lies in the assumption that UBI can substantially be paid for out of 'old money' – either by replacing a range of other benefits or at least by reducing entitlement to other benefits and transferring the resources to the new scheme. This chimes with a common view of UBI that it offers the opportunity to scrap everything and start again. That could lead to people on very low incomes being worse off, and most schemes have to moderate this aspiration in practice. Three of the schemes in Table 6.1 try to ensure that benefits are equivalent to, or better than, existing benefits.

---

[3] Citizens Income Trust (2015) 'Citizens income: a brief introduction', available at: http://www.citizensincome.org/wp-content/uploads/2016/03/Booklet2015.pdf

[4] The others in the table are from H. Reed and S. Lansley (2016) 'Universal basic income: an idea whose time has come?', Compass, available at: http://www.compassonline.org.uk/wp-content/uploads/2016/05/UniversalBasicIncomeByCompass-Spreads.pdf; Compass and Green Party (2015) 'Basic income: a detailed proposal', available at: https://policy.greenparty.org.uk/assets/files/Policy%20files/Basic%20Income%20Consultation%20Paper.pdf; Reform Scotland (2016) 'The basic income guarantee', available at: https://reformscotland.com/wp-content/uploads/2016/02/The-Basic-Income-Guarantee-1.pdf

Table 6.1: Some proposals for a basic income

	Citizens Income Trust Scheme A	Compass Scheme 2	Green Party	Reform Scotland
Level of benefit	£71.70 adult £56.80 children £56.80 adult under 25 £145.40 pensioner	£71 adult £59 children £61 adult under 25 £51 pensioner	£80 adult £50 child £180 pensioner £310 pensioner couple	£100 adult £50 child (Excludes pensioners)
Treatment of benefits	Abolition of State Pension, Pension Credit, tax credits, Child Benefit Transitional protection for pensioners	Abolition of Child Benefit Retention of other benefits UBI treated as income for means tests	Abolition of State Pension, Pension Credit, tax credits, Child Benefit	Abolition of Tax Credits, Child Benefit, JSA, Income Support, Universal Credit and some smaller benefits
Treatment of tax allowances	Abolition of personal tax allowance Removal of £10 billion of reliefs on private pensions contributions	Abolition of personal tax allowance	Abolition of personal tax allowance Removal of 44% of reliefs on private pensions contributions	Abolition of personal allowance
Treatment of National Insurance	Retention without benefits	Lower earnings limit reduced to zero; NICs levied on all earnings	Lower earnings limit reduced to zero; NICs levied on all earnings	Merger of NICs with tax system
Tax rate	No change	Basic 25% Higher 45% Top 50%	No change	Combined tax rates of 40%, 60% and 65%
Total cost	£278.5 billion	£209.5 billion	£331 billion	£247 billion

Note: NICs = National Insurance contributions.

If the Basic Income is less than the basic minimum currently provided by JSA, ESA or Universal Credit, those benefits would have to be retained. UBI would be directly deducted from some benefits – JSA, ESA and Income Support – and would reduce entitlement to a range of others, including Tax Credits, Universal Credit and Housing Benefit. That would save some money, but it would undermine many of the claimed advantages of UBI. There would still be a 'poverty trap': very high marginal rates of deduction would remain. Either Housing Benefit or Universal Credit would lead to the deduction of 65% of any further income.

The scope to raise 'new money' is also limited. After scrapping existing benefits, the main element in the finance depends on a substantial increase in personal taxation, usually combining high rates of income tax with increased National Insurance contributions (NICs) across a very wide range of income. Parts of this are illusory – what really matters is the income that people are left with. (It may be possible to keep some part of the expenditure off the books by allowing people to opt to take the income as a credit against their tax bill – effectively reconverting parts of the scheme back into a tax allowance.) However, further costs will also be incurred – most obviously, making transfer payments to people of working age who are neither part of the labour market nor currently provided for in the benefits system.

The most credible part of these proposals is that some of the necessary finance might be raised through addressing anomalies in the tax system – especially private pension relief and the upper limit on assessment for NICs. All the basic income schemes considered take it for granted that personal tax allowances can be abolished, and all income will be subject to tax and possibly NICs as well – but it would be difficult to justify the retention of contributions if they do not deliver any benefits. If, at the same time, tax allowances are removed completely, the system would lose its claim to be practical and minimally intrusive. All work done – including casual labour and payment taken cash in hand – would have to be reported to the authorities, properly recorded and accounted for. There seems to be an assumption here that work takes place in the formal economy, that an employer will always make a tax return, that people will know what money is coming in and how to report it in accounts (self-employed people often do not), and that the payment will be reported to the tax authority. The approach seems to be at odds with the stress on paying UBI as a way of recognising the precarious, uncertain status of work in general and low-paid work in particular. One of the strongest arguments for UBI is that it requires far less information and intrusiveness than other systems. If this is only to be achieved by farming out the discovery of the same information by tax collectors, it rather undermines that point.

The greatest weakness of all the schemes, however, is distributive. However it is done, UBI is going to command a substantial tranche of national resources. That is because it extends benefits to a large population, mainly better-off people of working age, which currently does not receive them. A Citizen's Income for people of working age must extend support to people on higher incomes. If the costs are held constant, poorer people must be worse off; if the costs increase, that increase has to be devoted substantially to those people on higher incomes. If people on low incomes are only getting partial replacements for the benefits that they already have, the benefits of UBI would be focused principally – and, in some cases, entirely – on the better-off. (This was true of Child Benefit for many years before the rules were changed to exempt it.) The key is to ensure that the finance of UBI is progressive – so that the gains to the better-off are offset by commensurately large increases to their contributions. However, as Reed and Lansley write, 'it is not possible to design a scheme that is revenue neutral, pays a decent sum and withdraws most means-tested benefits without significant numbers of losers'.[5]

Ian Gough has attacked Basic Income as 'deluded and diversionary':

[5] H. Reed and S. Lansley (2016) 'Universal basic income: an idea whose time has come?', Compass, p 22, available at: http://www.compassonline.org.uk/wp-content/uploads/2016/05/UniversalBasicIncomeByCompass-Spreads.pdf

What is achieved? A big cut in child poverty, yes, but tiny falls in pensioner and working age adult poverty, despite the latter being the basic goal of the policy. And the numbers reliant on means-testing will be cut by only one-fifth.[6]

To implement a UBI, the money has to go not to the bits of the system that most help people (getting money to people in need of support); not to straighten out the bits that do not help (usually because they do not pay enough); but to another purpose entirely. Some of the proposals begin by taking money away from people in need. The main Citizens Income Trust scheme threatens to subject more than a quarter of households in the lowest income decile to a cut in their income of more than 10%.[7] That is particularly hard to swallow.

This does not sink the principle of UBI altogether, but it is an argument for developing the approach more cautiously. A Basic Income would be a start, but it could only be a start. Income is only one way of providing goods and services, and benefits deal with many more issues than providing people with minimum funds. However the issues are approached, there will have to be a range of responses, and UBI can only ever be part of them. There should be scope, at least, for more universal benefits, and extending such benefits for children and older people in particular could do much to resolve the anomalies and insufficiency of current provision.

Some other ideas for reform

There are other big ideas for reform. One option was favoured by the Child Poverty Action Group (CPAG) for many years: it is to go 'back to Beveridge', putting much more emphasis on insurance-based

---

[6] I. Gough (2016) 'Potential benefits and pitfalls of a universal basic income', *Guardian*, available at: http://www.theguardian.com/politics/2016/jun/10/potential-benefits-and-pitfalls-of-a-universal-basic-income

[7] Citizens Income Trust (2015) 'Citizens income: a brief introduction', p 10, Table 2, available at: http://www.citizensincome.org/wp-content/uploads/2016/03/Booklet2015.pdf

benefits.[8] This is still the position of Frank Field MP, once CPAG's director. Field argues that only insurance benefits avoid the peculiar disincentives to save or earn that arise from means-tested benefits. Insurance benefits are well understood; they take into account the need to raise finance; where they are used, they have a substantial impact on the level and security of people's income packages; and they have been particularly effective in Europe as a means of providing adequate benefits for older people. In their nature, however, they cannot deal with all the issues – there will always be people who do not qualify for assistance.

A second option is to increase the weight given to means-tested benefits. This has effectively been the choice of most governments since 1970. The Heath government introduced the predecessors of tax credits and Housing Benefit; the Fowler reviews in the mid-1980s emphasised the importance of 'targeting' benefits on people with lower incomes; and the tax credits scheme introduced under the Labour government extended means testing further. The strongest case for means testing is probably that it redistributes money directly from rich to poor, and it is important to recognise that increasing means-tested benefits is one of the most basic ways to improve the position of people with low incomes. Unfortunately, means testing does not work very well, and all the problems outlined in Chapter Three apply. Some of its problems are the problems of selectivity: the complexity of the system, the difficulty of defining boundaries, the problems of inappropriate exclusions and inclusions, and the issues of fraud and error. Some of the problems are intrinsic to means-testing: the rapid fluctuations that people experience in their incomes; the difficulty of defining income and capital; the problem of dealing equitably with different sizes and shapes of families and households; and the sheer difficulty of keeping track of things.

[8] A. Atkinson (1969) *Poverty in Britain and the reform of social security*, Cambridge: Department of Applied Economics, ch 7; but see G. Fimister and R. Lister (1980) *Social security: The case against contribution tests*, London: Child Poverty Action Group.

A third option is to put much more weight on universal benefits. Most schemes for a UBI suggest that if the same unconditional benefits were available to everyone, lots of other benefits would be unnecessary. That could work, in theory, for unemployment, students and low earners; it might work for pensioners and long-term sickness if they were to be dealt with on the same terms as the other groups. However, that still leaves at least five other categories that would not be dealt with – disability, housing, bereavement, children and provision for emergencies. That implies that any revised scheme is going to be mixed – a combination of several approaches – rather than unitary. There is scope to extend universality by increasing Child Benefit or by making the State Pension universal. Neither of those would achieve all possible objectives, but specific benefits do not need to achieve every objective: they need only to do things better than the present system. When Child Benefit is taken together with a minimum wage, it does something that neither element can do on its own: a minimum income for people in work, adjusted to the size of the family. When a basic universal pension is taken in conjunction with private pensions, it shifts the purpose of private pensions from providing a minimum income to supplementing the common foundation – something that the private sector, which otherwise leaves gaps, can do much more effectively than its presumed role in replacing public provision.

The problem with all schemes to simplify benefits is that something has to be sacrificed. Benefits have lots of aims. They cover lots of contingencies. People's lives are complicated. The simpler the benefit and the simpler the idea behind it, the more likely it is that one principle or another will have to go. Work for those who can? This is a harsh way to respond to bereavement. Payment according to need? That does not help people plan for retirement. Standard payments for disabilities, so that people with the same impairments get the same benefit? That would be very hard to explain to ex-services personnel – or, indeed, to the general public. It is often possible to gloss over differences by paying more to everyone, but cutting corners usually means that you are likely to drive over someone's toes.

This points to a different kind of reform: trying not to replace everything with one wonderful system, but rather to change the balance between benefits of different types. The aim should be not to provide the answer to every problem, but to make for fewer problems.

How to change the system of benefits: a manifesto for change

In *How social security works*,[9] I argued that what any reforms needed to do was to:

- *reduce insecurity* – slow down the rate of adjustment, standardising periods for payment, making benefits less conditional;
- *reduce complexity and error* – making benefits calculations independent of other benefits, avoiding transitional arrangements by buying out rights, using existing medical evidence; and
- *develop benefits that cover more contingencies*, rather than forcing people to apply for benefits that do not fit too well. Examples of the benefits that ought to exist, but do not exist, are benefits for long-term disability, early retirement, further and higher education, and social inclusion. Currently, people in those circumstances mainly have to claim ESA or JSA instead.

The scope for improvement is limited. Social security is beset with 'wicked' problems, problems that have no clear solution. They are constantly changing; tilting the balance in one direction is always liable to upset balances achieved in other places. Any attempt to change or improve social security benefits runs, usually fairly quickly, into two basic problems. The first is the 'laid table': people and politicians tend to accept that what is offered at present is what needs to be there. As soon as one starts to discuss a benefit that already exists, it becomes clear that it exists for a reason, that the reason was probably good enough to justify the introduction of the benefit in the first place, and that some people have come to rely on it. People need to have a safe,

[9]   P. Spicker (2011) *How social security works*, Bristol: The Policy Press.

secure, predictable system of benefits. Changing that system leads to disruption, and disruption leads to confusion, hardship and a sense of unfairness. Consider, for example, the unhappy experience of the 'bedroom tax', a wheeze cooked up by the Coalition government for saving some money on Housing Benefit by deducting payments to people deemed to be in properties bigger than they need, regardless of whether they have any other options. Housing Benefit is a clumsily designed benefit, which produces all kinds of unpredictable and undesired effects – including the creation of a class of private landlords paid inconsistent, arbitrarily negotiated sums by benefits authorities. That does not mean that, once it is in place, the benefit can easily be reformed in any direction, and a series of political protests have been devoted to keeping things as they were before the latest change.

The second problem, which is just as deeply entrenched, is the 'zero-sum game'. Benefits as they are now cost a substantial amount of money. Governments do not want to pay more, and they find it difficult to pay less. What happens, then, if they want to make a particular group better off? As a simple matter of mathematics, if the budget stays the same, and one person is better off, then someone else is going to have to be worse off. The current distinction between Personal Independence Payment and Attendance Allowance, which arbitrarily denies mobility assistance to some older people with disabilities and not to others, is unsustainable. The moral case for extending mobility support to older people is hard to resist – but there is no way of doing this without getting the money from somewhere else. That leads to a general observation in the formation of social security policy: *every change in the rules either costs money or leaves someone worse off*. The only way to reform benefits without pain is to spend more.

This book has laid out arguments for a radically different direction of movement from most of the things that have been done in social security policy for the last fifty years. The dominant themes of policy have been:

- simplification: the belief that the system can be stripped down, rationalised and streamlined;
- personalisation: the focus on the individual characteristics and needs of the claimant;
- selectivity: the attempt to develop benefits that focus resources on those in need and deny benefits to others;
- activation: the focus on work; and
- conditionality: the attempt to change behaviour through the conditions imposed on benefit receipt.

The approaches I have advocated are substantially opposed to those themes:

- *Managed complexity.* The first difference concerns simplification. Most people would agree that the benefits system needs to be simpler; there are points in the course of the argument where I have said the same. Many of the attempts to simplify the system, such as lumping little benefits together into bigger benefits, have been self-defeating, and some measures that have been presented as rationalisations, such as the stripped-down focus on work associated with 'welfare reform', have simply been destructive. Any reform of benefits needs to accept that the benefit system is complicated for good reasons: that it is trying to do many things, that the aims are complicated and that people's lives are complicated. The method must be based not on simplification, but on managing complexity.

  Most of the detailed proposals that I have made are attempts to make complex situations more manageable. This follows a general principle in problem solving: if a problem is too big to solve, the thing to do is to break it down into smaller problems, and to keep on breaking it down until the problems that are left are small enough to be tackled. The system of social security has been infected by a misplaced confidence in technical solutions: if only they can sort out the computer systems, go for bigger benefits or get the information in, then everything should work. It never does. Instead of trying to define great big benefits and tweak them to adapt them all to individual circumstances, it makes more sense to define smaller benefits that can be added up in different ways for different people. Income is fungible. If benefit packages are stitched together from a range of different sources, then each of the benefits can contribute towards a stable income, but the income will differ with different entitlements. The trick is to pay the benefits all on the same day so that the variations do not lead to administrative hassle and uncertainty for each and every benefit.

- *Rights.* Individualised responses depend on the misplaced confidence that the administration is capable of keeping track of the finer detail of people's lives. Benefits need, to some degree, to be impersonal – constant, reliable, predictable and insensitive to personal difference. The more they vary, the more difficult it becomes to cope with the complexity of people's lives.

The argument for rights is often expressed in moral terms, but for present purposes, it is no less important that it also describes a series of mechanisms. Rights define expectations and the conduct of the administration. They are not subject to arbitrary judgement. They are enforceable. Personalisation calls for fine judgement; rights require conformity with rules and consistent practice. The most effective arguments for benefits have been based on the rights of citizenship, rather than the needs of the individual, because those rights are held in common by everyone, and they justify a more broadly based, less discriminatory approach. The argument for rights is an argument for consistency, predictability and security. We have to respond less to personal need and more to people's rights.

- *Recognising the diverse role of benefits.* A key part of the argument of this book has been a plea to recognise that benefits do many things, and that their aims stand to be compromised by the imposition of external criteria. The idea of welfare reform has centrally focused on the misconception that benefits must be dedicated to getting people into work. Most benefits have nothing to do with work, and it would be helpful to think in different terms entirely. For those benefits concerned with periods without work – principally JSA and parts of ESA – they need to be uncoupled from personalised employment support. The benefits are worse for having those elements, and those elements are worse for being tied to the benefits system.

- *Minimal presumption.* One of the recurring themes of this book has been the misplaced presumption behind many policies – the demand that benefits agencies know everything, judge everything and act on everything. The same thread runs through the objections to selectivity, information management and conditionality. It is hardly possible to avoid the issues altogether, but it is at least possible to reduce the burden. No system can operate effectively for millions of people while attempting to subject the individuals within it to a detailed scrutiny of their circumstances, conduct and merits. Benefits need to assume less, demand less and work with less.

There are several routes by which changes can be brought about:

- There may be alternatives to using benefits at all. Free prescriptions, introduced in Scotland, are one example; free food in hospitals is another. There are times when it makes more sense to deliver the goods than to pay people cash benefits to buy them. Public subsidies for housing – the system prior to the development of Housing Benefit – were more effectively used to supply housing than the current system is.
- There are alternative ways of developing and constructing benefits – for example, linking disability compensation with accident claims in the courts (the system in New Zealand), or paying benefits in principle to children rather than adult carers (France). A large number of benefits have been tried in the past – an insurance-based Death Grant, benefits for lone parents, benefits for severe disability, early retirement benefits and so on. Things do not have to be the way they are now.
- Benefits can be combined differently. Many of the problems of coordination stem from interactions between alternative benefits and the effect that claiming one benefit has on entitlement to others. Benefits can be treated as a fungible part of an income

package, so long as they do not interact in this way. There is a good case for using several smaller benefits in combination; there is no advantage in holding to the conventional (and potentially catastrophic) preference for big, portmanteau benefits.

- Benefits can be administered differently. It needs to be questioned whether entitlements have to depend on the initiative of the claimant. Technology can be used to expand the ways that service users interact with the system, rather than closing down face-to-face or phone contact. Officials can use the technology to guide users through difficult processes, which is the way it works in France – a *technicien* will have a screen positioned to be shared with the claimant at the other side of the desk.
- The criteria on which benefits are delivered can be diversified. There is no reason for everyone who claims a sickness benefit to have an individual assessment, and for most, the assessments that they have had as part of their health care are enough. Systems of review cannot be avoided, but they can be done in different ways and the burden on service users can be reduced.
- Unfair rules can be changed – for example, the shocking breaches of natural justice associated with sanctions. Social security agencies have to be reconfigured to learn from their mistakes. There have to be systems to allow bad practice to be challenged; that implies rapid and accessible mechanisms for managing complaints, internal scrutiny and judicial review.

It has to be admitted that pleas for benefits to become more impersonal or to adapt to complexity do not promise to be among the great rallying cries for future reform. This is not an inspirational book. Its proposals for change may not be as exciting as big ideas like a Citizen's Income or Universal Credit. They would not resolve all the issues. However, they could at least reduce the range and number of problems that have to be dealt with, and that is better than doing nothing. Benefits can be different, and they should be.

Index